# Claire King

# Claire King
## Confessions of a Bad Girl

With Neil Howarth

920
---
KIN

JOHN BLAKE

Published by John Blake Publishing Ltd,
3 Bramber Court, 2 Bramber Road,
London W14 9PB, England

www.blake.co.uk

First published in hardback in 2006

ISBN 1 84454 253 X

British Library Cataloguing-in-Publication Data:

A catalogue record for this book is available from the British Library.

Design by www.envydesign.co.uk

Printed in Great Britain by Creative Print and Design, Wales

1 3 5 7 9 10 8 6 4 2

Papers used by John Blake Publishing are natural, recyclable products
made from wood grown in sustainable forests. The manufacturing processes
conform to the environmental regulations of the country of origin.

Every attempt has been made to contact the relevant copyright-holders,
but some were unobtainable. We would be grateful if the appropriate people
could contact us.

To Mum and Dad for Being Just That

## ACKNOWLEDGEMENTS

First of all, my thanks to Mum and Dad. Your support and unconditional love throughout my life have meant the world to me, as do you both. You've been there for me throughout everything, and I mean everything. Now it's my turn to be there for you. To my brother Piers, for being the person he is and the person he helped me become – cheers for the laughs. To Peter, for giving me some of the best years of my life. To my best friends across the world (stop moving so far away from me!) – you all know who you are – it wouldn't have been the same without you, and neither would this book. I love you *all*. And last but certainly not least, to my co-author Neil – I couldn't have done this without you and I certainly wouldn't have done it with anyone else. You've become a true friend – and now know more than you should! But the job's a good 'un. Thanks again and big love, Claire.

And not forgetting my beloved Digger – the only male who's never let me down. But then again, he doesn't know where I keep his chewies.

The quiet hog always eats...

# Contents

# If a Job's Worth Doing…

Over the years, I've been invited to 'spill the beans' many times and I've always said no. So why am I doing it now? Well, I've had to face the harsh reality, especially more recently, that, if you don't put your own story across, someone else's version will be taken as gospel – when that's really not the case at all. So, I decided the time was finally right to set the record straight. When you've spent most of your professional life trying to keep your personal life *personal*, that can be a very uncomfortable task. But, as my parents have always said, 'If a job's worth doing, it's worth doing properly.' Hopefully, that's what I've done here: told it like it is.

If some people had had their way, though, I might never have been here at all. Dad, a newly commissioned army officer, and Mum, a secretary at a local music emporium, were unmarried and barely out of their teens when the shock announcement of my imminent arrival was made. A grandchild born 'the wrong side of the sheets' wasn't a prospect that delighted their parents, but the suggestion that an abortion was 'an easy way out' was less than well received by mine, who were very much in love and determined to have their child. So, the following summer, after winning my grandparents' blessing and the army's permission, I secretly attended my parents' wedding.

As for the rest of my life so far: it's been exciting, heartbreaking, terrifying and testing – but never dull.

# Prologue

The moment I saw Bob Geldof in the flesh I knew I wanted him. This surprised me, as I hadn't fancied him at all in any of the band's videos or posters, but he was definitely gorgeous in real life.

The year was 1979 and I was with my friend Fiona at a Boomtown Rats gig at the Manchester Apollo. The Rats were quite big, having just had hits with 'Mary of the Fourth Form' and 'Rat Trap', but they weren't as massive as they would go on to be and the gig was fairly low-key. Fiona and I had all their records and bought tickets to see them as soon as we heard about the gig.

The band were amazing, and as Geldof worked the crowd I felt a surge of electricity running through my body. I knew I was witnessing something special and I couldn't take my eyes off him.

When the show ended, we made our way to the bar and

noticed lots of girls desperately trying to get backstage. Even though we'd hoped to catch a glimpse of the boys, we didn't want to stand with the groupies, so we decided to leave. We were just about to exit a side door when a dark-haired guy came over to us, asking whether we'd like to go backstage for a drink. We looked at each other and then Fiona asked him who he was to make sure it wasn't a wind-up. He introduced himself as Robbie McGrath, the Boomtown Rats' tour manager. We still played it cool, saying, 'Why not?' and followed him.

As he led us towards the stage entrance, we made excited faces at each other behind his back and then smiled smugly at the girls begging to be allowed backstage as we were guided past them. When we reached the backstage bar, Robbie told us to help ourselves to a drink and said the boys would be through in a minute. Over at the little bar, in the corner of what was a dingy-looking room with a few old chairs and tables that had definitely seen better days scattered around, we fixed ourselves large vodka and Cokes.

The band turned up a few minutes later, followed by a selection of girls who'd obviously also been invited in from the audience. In fact, there were now more than enough females to match the boys, and it annoyed us a bit that Robbie had invited a lot more backstage than just us. 'I know we really like them, but let's just have a drink and go,' Fiona said to me. 'We don't want to look desperate like that lot, do we?'

I nodded, as the gaggle of girls, who were practically

kissing the band's arses, got louder and louder. 'That way if they *really* like us they'll invite us to another gig,' she said. I agreed with her, so, after mingling with the lads for about ten minutes, we finished our drinks and grabbed our bags.

'Right, we're off. Have fun, boys,' I told them, winking in the direction of Geldof, who'd caught my eye several times. It was then that I realised just how gorgeous he was. Tall, dark and unusually handsome, he had beautiful brown eyes and his smile sent shivers down my spine. But I wasn't hanging around for anyone and I certainly wasn't going to be part of a pack.

We were walking to the door when Pete Briquette, the bass player, came over to us. 'Why are you leaving so early?' he asked.

'Seems like there's more than enough girls willing to keep you lot happy,' I told him. 'And if the boys really want to get to know us we'll see you at the next gig – if we're invited.' I scribbled down our numbers and handed them to him, and with that we walked off laughing. I desperately wanted to turn round and have another look at Geldof but I managed not to – just. Little did I know that the adventure was only just beginning …

# 1

# In The Beginning

It was on my fourth birthday that I realised I wasn't going to be a typical 'girly girl'. As a special treat, Mum had organised a party and had a very delicate party dress made for me. I'll never forget that dress: it was bright red with ruffles around the neck and was covered in bows. Mum had apparently been made to wear a similar one at the same age and I would later find out that this was her revenge!

I was made to show off my new dress by twirling around in the middle of the room as the other girls and their mothers oohed and aahed. I was on my second twirl and just thinking how horribly itchy it was, when, out of the window, I spotted Dad and my little brother Piers working in the garden.

Thinking how much more fun it looked out there, I pretended I was going to the loo and tiptoed quietly outside. It was a lovely sunny day and our black Labrador, Kim, was running around, as Dad dug holes for plants he was putting in the flowerbeds. 'Can I help?' I asked in my best 'don't say no' voice, the one I used around Christmas time.

Dad turned round to me with a look of mischief on his face. 'I don't think your mum would be too pleased, would she?' he said, but it was too late to stop me. I'd already picked up a trowel and was kneeling in the earth digging a hole. Dad just rolled his eyes. At this point, Mum's voice rang out from the doorway: 'Claire! *What* are you doing?'

I turned to her, trowel in hand, new dress covered with mud. 'Digging,' I said, probably sounding rather pleased with myself.

At this, she gave Dad a filthy look and hurried down the steps. 'Little girls don't play in the mud, Claire. Don't you want to come and play Pass the Parcel with the other girls?' Mum must have noticed that it was obvious I didn't want to come inside, as before I could answer she stepped towards me and said in a low voice, loud enough for me to understand she was not happy but not loud enough for the guests indoors to hear, 'Look at the mess you've made of your lovely dress. All the good girls are playing nicely inside, Claire. Only boys and naughty girls play in the dirt, and you don't want to be a bad girl now, do you?'

'Oh yes I do,' I said and went on digging.

Mum looked at me despairingly, shrugged, then walked back towards the house muttering something about my dress. Dad winked at me and threw me a bigger trowel.

I'll never know what made me say what I said, but all I knew was that, if being a bad girl meant I could play in the mud instead of twirling around like a Barbie doll in an itchy party dress, then that's what I was going to be.

Mum and Dad were very much the good cop/bad cop duo, with Mum normally the good one. We could get away with murder with her but you knew you were in trouble if you got on the wrong side of Dad. He could be fun at times, but he wasn't a father who really played with us. He didn't kick a football about with Piers, and I rarely remember him playing games with us – apart from with the Scalextric he'd bought me for my fourth birthday, which was clearly more for him to play with, but I enjoyed watching the cars whizzing by anyway.

But he did teach us to swim – apparently by throwing us into the water at nine months old! – and we both went on to become strong swimmers, with Piers even getting into *The Guinness Book of Records* for playing in the longest water-polo match.

Occasionally, Dad would buy us presents when he came back from working away. He was an only child and was never given presents, just money to buy his own. I think his own childhood was one of 'tough love', so he didn't know how to treat us, but he did spoil us in other ways. He would often take the family to Ibiza, where his good friend Graham Hill, the world champion Formula One driver, and his family holidayed. On one trip, I was caught running naked along the beach with their son Damon. We were only four, though!

A tactile family we weren't. Dad didn't really do

cuddles; that was Mum's department. If I fell over in front of him, he *might* have picked me up and said something like, 'Oh, you'll be all right. Now pull yourself together and carry on playing.' Whereas Mum would immediately be smothering me with lovely cuddles, saying, 'Let's get you to the bathroom and put some Germolene on.' Germolene was one of Mum's 'must haves' – there were tubes of it all over the house and whenever I smell it now it always takes me back.

All in all, we rubbed along quite nicely as a family, and Piers and I – he is 18 months younger – got on really well. Because our house was miles away from any neighbours, we had only each other to play with, so that probably helped make us even closer. We had to get on – otherwise, you had to play alone. Naturally, we'd have spats every now and again over silly things, but not as bad as your average siblings, and we spent a lot of time together just playing happily.

Sunday mornings always used to be 'tea and biscuits time' in our parents' bedroom. One Sunday, we'd been sitting in my brother's room, which was always a tip – I must have been about eight and Piers six – and it was a little later than we'd normally be called in to join them, so we decided to go to their room for our treat.

Piers went first, with me chasing him along the corridor, and when he got to their bedroom door he opened it and ran straight in, me right behind him. As soon as we were inside, Dad starting screaming at us to get out, as Mum frantically pulled the sheets over them. We didn't know

4

what was going on (although I assumed they must have been having a kiss and a cuddle – I knew mums and dads did this as we'd talked about it at school – and also I couldn't see any tea and biscuits) but we knew we were in big trouble because Dad was shouting at us in the voice he used when he was seriously mad.

Slipping out of the room first, I heard Piers, who must have been rooted to the spot with fear, get the blame for not knocking. Dad marched him back to his room; he must have seen me, I thought. Damn! He told us to get dressed and then left us alone for what seemed like ages.

We were both starting to hope that that was that, when he came back saying, 'Right, you two – outside now.' We followed him downstairs and into the garden, both quite frightened. He sent Piers to one end of the drive and me to the other, saying we had to weed it until we met in the middle as punishment for not knocking. It was an absolutely freezing winter's day and as the drive was at least 90 feet long we were wondering how long we'd have to stay out there. After about an hour, Mum must have felt sorry for us, as she came out, brought us inside and then prepared breakfast while Dad made hawk's eyes at us over his paper. We both knew we would never again go into their bedroom without knocking first.

Even though Dad was what you'd call strict, I was definitely a daddy's girl.

We used to have a big fireplace in our house in Bishop Thornton, near Harrogate, and above the log fire was a little group of Mum's favourite bits and pieces, along with her collection of riding whips and pill boxes. I used to love looking at all her 'special things' but my favourite was definitely the onyx cigarette box – it was so shiny. Next to it sat an onyx lighter.

I noticed that when my parents threw parties (in the late 1960s and 1970s, having dinner parties at your home was 'the thing to do') this fascinating box was where all the grown-ups got their cigarettes from, and I used to watch them from behind the curtains, thinking how much I wanted to be like them. I decided that if I smoked a cigarette from the onyx box it might make me grow up quickly, so whenever people weren't around I used to sneak in, take a cigarette and have a puff or two.

Now, this probably sounds like quite normal teenage behaviour, but the big difference was that I was five years old. In my little mind, the grown-ups were all smoking, and I thought it looked good. I'll have a go at that, I decided. So I got into the habit of helping myself, and whenever I'd finished a cigarette I'd put the butt in an antique copper kettle that stood by the fireplace and which I'd been told not to play with. No one uses that kettle, I said to myself, so, if I hide them in there, no one will know. Only I was wrong.

Mrs Elsworth, our home help, must have found them one day, because on my way down the stairs that afternoon I overheard Mum telling Dad that I'd been smoking and him replying, in his 'definitely not happy actually' voice, that I 'must be spoken to – immediately'. Panicking, I ran back upstairs and into my bedroom, closing the door firmly behind me. I was sitting on the bed, really beginning to worry, and considering hiding in the wardrobe, when Mum flung open the door and said I had to come down to the sitting room as my father wanted to speak to me.

Downstairs, Dad was sitting at one end of the table and his face had that purple tint he got in his cheeks when he'd been shouting. Now I was definitely worried. He told me to sit opposite him and said that everyone knew I'd been smoking their cigarettes and I would be better off just admitting it before matters got any worse. Knowing I was in serious trouble, I tried to deny it and suggested that, as it wasn't me, maybe it was someone else. Now, although I didn't actually say it was Piers, I kept on saying it wasn't me, while Dad insisted, 'Well, it's either you or Piers' – and obviously it wasn't Piers. He was only three!

He kept on shouting at me to admit what I'd done, so in the end I just dropped my head and confessed. Once I'd owned up, Dad seemed a bit less agitated. Mum got up from the table, leaving him to do the speaking, as always. Once she'd gone, I knew anything could happen. I just kept my head down and hoped for the best.

Moments later, out of the corner of my eye, I saw Dad get up from the table. I lifted my head up and watched as he walked over to the onyx cigarette box. He picked it up, carried it over to me and placed it on the table. 'So you like smoking then, do you, Claire?' he said, leaning towards me. 'Well, if you want to smoke like grown-ups, then you'll have to practise, as grown-ups don't smoke a little bit of a cigarette and then hide it in a kettle, Claire,' he said rather heartily. 'Grown-ups smoke whole packs, so that's what you can do – now.'

Dad looked at me with amusement. I think he thought I was going to cry and be scared to smoke in front of him, but his challenge simply made me stretch out my little hand for the cigarette box. His shocked eyes stayed on me as I reached for the lighter, put a cigarette in my mouth and lit it almost defiantly.

By now, I felt certain he was about to hit me, but I smoked the cigarette as best as I could and when it was finished I put it in the ashtray and looked up at him. Giving me a strange look, he gestured at me to smoke another, but I was just putting out my hand for one when he suddenly closed the box and started laughing. I wasn't sure why, but I hoped it was a good sign.

He leaned over again and said quietly, 'I got caught smoking when I was five as well.' Then he winked and said I could go and play. I walked off completely at a loss as to why he wasn't angry with me any more, but in hindsight I can see that we seemed to click over that cigarette. I think maybe Dad liked the fact that I seemed to rise to the challenge – even though it was supposed to be a punishment. And after that I was always more of a daddy's girl, because I was like him – mischievous and up for the craic.

My parents, Angela Catherine Wilson and John Charles Seed, were quite different but seemed to really gel as a couple. Every Christmas, we'd have a party and a few members of my mother's side of the family would come over. Dad's parents retired to Torquay and as they never liked to travel much we very rarely saw them.

First to arrive would be Great-Grandmother Wilson, along with my maternal grandparents Ella and Lesley Wilson. Great-Grandmother Wilson was a large, ferocious-looking woman in her eighties who wouldn't have been out of place in a Dickens novel. When she rolled into the living room in her wrought-iron wheelchair you'd have to move out of her way quickly, otherwise she'd crush your toes with relish. Although she was a pleasant enough woman, Piers and I used to hate her coming at Christmas because A: the presents she gave us were always unwanted ones she'd previously received and she hadn't even bothered to take off the gift tags addressed to her. And B: she had quite a decent moustache, so being told to kiss her hello was quite out of the question. Piers and I would hide away to avoid that situation whenever possible.

Next to turn up would be my uncle Peter and his wife, Elaine. He is Mum's younger brother and had a beard that was rather fitting for Christmas. He'd lost the hearing in one ear in a car crash in his teens, so from a child's point of view it was like having a deaf Father Christmas there. He could be really funny, though, and invented a game called Puff Puff. He would make Piers and me eat flaky cheese biscuits, then hang us upside down and make us say, 'Puff, puff', which sprayed the remnants everywhere. It was a game Great-Grandma Wilson found less than charming. Aunt Elaine was as skinny as my grandma was round. She wore very heavy eye make-up and seemed to be stuck in the hippy sixties. I liked Elaine; she was funny and enjoyed dancing around to Christmas jingles.

After dinner – Mum's Christmas dinners are still second to none and a traditional six courses – it was cheese and port time. You had to pass the port the correct way – to the left – and you got a right rollicking if you didn't. A few drinks in, Dad would start telling blue stories, at which Mum would laugh but always look embarrassed. She has never really liked to be the focus of attention, whereas Dad is happy taking centre stage, telling rude jokes or funny stories. I used to love listening to him when he was on a roll, with everyone hanging on his every word as he told some tale or other. Sometimes they would talk about the family's backgrounds at these get-togethers, the way older people do.

The Seed and Wilson clans were both well-to-do, although they were from different parts of the social spectrum. 'You do know your mother's side of the family is related to Sir Francis Drake, don't you, Claire?' Grandma Ella would remind us all from her side of the table. I would nod politely, as Dad rolled his eyes; I'd heard her stories before – every year! Grandpa Leslie, her husband, would recount the time when, at three years old, I happened upon his glass of evening sherry and downed the lot while he was getting ready for a black-tie do. Things like that were not quickly forgotten in our household.

Grandpa Leslie's family owned textile mills in Yorkshire, but Grandma – Ella Wilson, née Drake – could trace her family tree back to Sir Francis. So, to put it frankly, Mum's family had a touch of the la-di-das while Dad was from more of a vagabond tribe. His family were middle-class with an edge: they were of a good mix of Yorkshire and Irish stock. Dad's grandmother was from Kenmare, in County Kerry, and her ancestry could be traced back – according to my father's father, Grandpa Charlie – to Scottish horse thieves who raided England in the 15th century. He stopped tracing the lineage any further, as it was too embarrassing.

The Seeds and the Wilsons lived in the same part of West Yorkshire. Both my grandfathers were rugby captains, Charlie Seed for Bradford and Yorkshire and Leslie Wilson for Morley, so they had something in common. My grandmothers were less alike. Kathleen Seed, my dad's mother, apparently felt inferior at family get-togethers but I don't know why, as his side were quite well-to-do in a West Yorkshire way. The Seeds were maltsters – they changed barley into malt for brewing and distilling.

Anyway, back to my immediate family. I was born six and half months after my parents married and Piers came along a year and a half later. Our first family house, where my parents would end up living for 40 years, was Roseberry Cottage, so called because, behind it in the distance, you could see Roseberry Topping, with its carved white horse. We all loved our home, which had five bedrooms, a swimming pool, stables and 16 acres of land. The only trouble was that as there were no neighbours there was never anyone else to play with unless Piers and I brought friends home from West End, the private junior school in Harrogate which both of us attended.

While I loved my brother, school was where I got to meet other girls, and it was nice to be able to play with them for a change. There I instantly made friends with Vicky Farnell, a pretty blonde girl who seemed to giggle at the same things as me. We always sat together and were soon joined by Caroline Bostock, who lived the closest to my house – at five miles away. And then there was Caroline Cowling, known as Carty, who loved ponies almost as much as I did. We all quickly became firm friends and were even chosen by a local photographer to pose together for a newspaper picture on the Stray, a lovely area in the centre of Harrogate that helps it to win 'the most beautiful town' competitions time and again.

Mum would drive us to and from school in her open-top Triumph Vitesse. No seatbelts were worn back then and straw hats were often lost to the wind. She couldn't really have been a better mother than she was: one day when we were running late, she even drove us there in her nightie. She was soft and caring, made our favourite dinners all the time and took us shopping.

Dad, however, rarely seemed to be at home, as he had to travel a lot on business. After the family concern was sold, his next job took him to Inverness, but he was always home at weekends. So Piers and I would get away with playing up all week and when Dad came home we'd be as good as gold, for fear of being shouted at. Poor Mum, she really did have her work cut out, especially when Piers developed a kidney infection that made him so ill that he was hospitalised and operated on, and they thought we might lose him.

Fortunately, he recovered well and would later tell anyone who'd listen that the scar around his middle was from a shark bite. I think Mum enjoyed staying at home with us, as she never ventured out to work until we both started boarding school. She was happy to be a stay-at-home mum until then, and we were happy to have her.

When Piers was sent, at eight years old, to a prep school called Bramcote, I was really sad to see him go. We'd always been close, so it was upsetting to hear that I would only be seeing him in the holidays. I really felt like I'd lost my best buddy. To try to cheer me up, my parents finally said I could have my own pony. On hearing the news, I shamefully admit, I was so excited that I waved Piers off rather merrily. For as long as I could remember, I'd wanted a pony but had always been told I wasn't old enough to look after one properly.

I argued and argued that I was responsible enough to have one, saying that since we lived in the country and had so much land, keeping a pony was not going to be a problem, and eventually I won the argument. My ninth birthday wasn't long after Piers left, and my surprise present was a gorgeous pure-white 'grey' called Rocket. I'd gone with Mum to see a friend of hers who had a pony for sale, apparently because her daughter had outgrown him. It turned out that he was being sold by Tommy Stack, who had won the Grand National on Red Rum and since retiring had become a successful trainer. Tommy was a friend of the family and they had asked him to help them sell the pony.

It wasn't long after I fell in love with Rocket that I found another male competing for my affections. Robert Booth and I were both ten and at school together. I thought he was lovely; he had blond hair and was very sporty. Even the fact that his dad was a pig farmer seemed romantic! It was terribly innocent and we used to play 'kiss catch' in the Oval, a huge green area filled with trees.

Robert was always nice and would bring sweets into school for me. Once we were passing one of those 'tick the box if you love me' pieces of paper under the desks when our teacher caught us and gave us both letters to take home telling our parents why we weren't concentrating in class.

One Friday lunchtime, Robert asked if I wanted to go to the local cinema with him to watch the latest Herbie movie, *The Love Bug*, at the Saturday matinee. When I asked Mum, she said she'd have to ask my father later, and when she did I heard him tell her, 'Absolutely no way.' Running into the living room and bursting into tears, I pleaded with them to let me go and even said they could come with us. Dad remained absolutely resolute and by now I was so upset I couldn't stop crying. Why wouldn't they let me go with Robert? They would have let me if he had been a girl. The sad thing was that it was so innocent – we'd only wanted to see a kids' film.

Knowing that Dad was not for turning and realising that boys were going to be a tricky subject with my parents from now on, I gave in and asked if I could go with my friend Carty. They agreed and the following day they dropped me off at the cinema, where I promptly snuck round the back and met Robert. What they don't know..., I thought, as I held Robert's hand in the front row and we shared a bag of sweets.

After that, we started hanging around together on the quiet. I loved spending time with Robert but we never did anything other than hold hands and kiss – with our mouths closed, of course.

By now, I was doing well in school and had started winning public-speaking competitions all over Yorkshire – it seemed my weekly elocution lessons were paying off. Mum had been suffering from a bad back, so she stayed at home while Dad took me to competition after competition and we grew even closer. My string of successes gave me confidence and a taste for performing in public. And it made me think about what I might like to do in the future. I didn't know what that might be, but I knew that it wouldn't be a nine-to-five job. Already, though, plans were being made for my future.

One night, after I'd been out with Rocket, I was called to the sitting room. It was odd, because Dad was at home in the week, which meant he must have taken the day off work. Immediately I expected the worst, though it turned out I hadn't done anything wrong. Oh no, what's happened? I thought, as they asked me to sit down and started telling me they had something to talk to me about.

My stomach was really in knots as I sat there waiting.

'You're eleven now, Claire, and next week, when it's time to go back to school, you'll be boarding at Harrogate Ladies' College,' Dad told me.

I cried and cried when I heard that I was being sent away. It shouldn't have been such a shock, as Piers had already been away for three years. But the thought hadn't crossed my mind that girls also went away to boarding school, and since I'd been so busy with Rocket during the school holidays I'd forgotten that I wouldn't be going back to West End. I looked at them both. Mum was crying. I was told it would be 'good for you' and I knew by now that when it came to Dad's decisions there was no point in protesting.

So, a week later, I said my goodbyes to Rocket, my special boy, and at the end of the summer break I was driven the seven miles to my new school.

'Surely I could be a day girl,' I said, as it was so close.

'No,' came the answer.

I didn't feel well in the car but I knew this would sound like an excuse not to go, so I sat in silence as I was taken away to what seemed like prison.

Not long after bedding down in the dorm, I suddenly felt really ill. I was taken to see the nurse and then the local doctor, who referred me to a specialist paediatrician called Dr Paddy Clarke. After examining me, he called my parents, who were friends of his, to say I had suspected rheumatic fever *and* a heart murmur, which is an irregular heartbeat. I was scared when I heard Dr Clarke say this on the phone, but when he added, 'She'll have to come back home for quite some time,' I felt instantly better.

Mum collected me, with lots of hugs and kisses, and took me home to rest. Once there, all excitement soon disappeared as I became very ill. I was constantly being sick and had what felt like really bad flu. Mum was great, never leaving my side. The doctor put me on lots of medicines and after a while I didn't feel ill any more, but I was told that I had to stay away from school because, unless I rested properly, I would relapse.

This was the start of quite a strange time for me, because, although I didn't know how ill I was, I knew it had to be quite serious for me to be taken out of school. I was kept at home for about six months and mainly stayed in bed reading, though sometimes I was allowed to go out on Rocket. A lot of the time, I would lie there dreaming of being a famous pop star and travelling all over the world. Being on my own at home so much made me feel more independent and able to enjoy my own company. Ultimately, it did me good, as I learned to depend on myself. I grew up quite a lot lying in that bed day after day. Eventually, I recovered completely and went back to boarding school 100 per cent fit.

Because I'd been stuck at home so long, I suddenly relished the freedom that boarding school brought and was soon having fun with the other girls in my room. We'd have midnight feasts and sing with our hairbrushes, while practising dance routines in the mirror and, of course, swoon over the latest pop stars like Donny Osmond.

Everybody fancied Donny. Elvis Presley and Kenny Dalglish were also up there on my piece of wall. They were more my style as they seemed to have a bit of an edge to them, and I realised then that I liked my boys a bit less goody-goody. In fact, Elvis, aka 'The King' would later be the inspiration for my stage name when I found out that there was already a Claire Seed in Equity.

Talking of boys, which we did nearly all the time, some of the boarders from nearby Ashville Boys College would stand outside at night, whistling up at our windows. The bolder ones even climbed on to our balconies. Half-terrified, half-excited, the screams of teenage girls could be heard throughout the corridors, and, just as the bravest of us were about to open the windows, the matron, Mrs French, or our house mistress, Mrs Ireland, would sweep into our rooms, sending drooling girls dashing for their beds, as she shouted to the boys that they'd called the police.

With the hormones flowing everywhere, lesbianism was also rife. We suspected in particular a couple of teachers who often did the midnight rounds, and there was definitely a bit of experimentation going on in some of the smaller dormitory rooms. The biggest dorms had six beds and some of the smaller ones two or three.

One night, I'd just come out of the bathroom and was brushing my hair, when one of the girls asked me to come and sit on her bed. I didn't think anything of it and went over and sat next to her, imagining she was going to tell me about some boy she liked.

'Claire, do you know how to French kiss?' she asked in a tone that immediately made me feel uneasy.

'Why?' I said cautiously, gently shuffling my bottom a little further away from her.

'Well,' she said slowly, 'it's good to practise – so you get it right.' She moved a little closer. 'Come here and I'll show you how to do it properly,' she added, pushing towards me.

I stood up instantly and started walking back towards the bathroom. 'No thanks,' I said, as I reached the door. 'I know what to do.'

'But I wanted to tell you about the facts of life, Claire,' she whined after me.

I ignored her, stepped into the bathroom and locked the door. Honestly – as if! I thought, as I started brushing my hair. I knew what she was up to. I was 13 by now and not as green as she'd hoped – being at an all-girls' school, you soon learned what was what.

And I'd already had the 'birds and the bees' chat from my dad, who'd sat me and Piers down on a recent weekend trip home. I wasn't surprised it was Dad that gave us 'the chat', as Mum wasn't into that sort of conversation. If you needed straight facts, Dad was your man. Luckily, Mum had included a brief mention of periods, so I was one of the lucky few who could calm down the less informed girls who, shocked at starting their first period, would run around the dorm screaming things like, 'What's happening to me – am I dying?'

Boarding-school life was never dull and, although I had

my sad moments when I would write 'bring me home' letters to my parents, on the whole I'd started to enjoy it and had made a really good friend in Fiona McKie, who was from the same village, loved horses and was also a boarder. We'd also meet up in the holidays and ride together.

One time when I was at home, Mum, who had decided to set up a shop in Harrogate called Country Life, to sell riding and shooting equipment, had asked me to help out on the day that the top show-jumper Harvey Smith was to open it. My job was to collect the glasses at the champagne reception. When I noticed that lots of them were not quite empty I quietly decanted the leftovers into my own hidden glass and by the end of the day I was more than a little tipsy!

Even though I was enjoying school more, I still always looked forward to going home whenever we had a break. On one trip home, I was devastated to find my beloved Rocket had been sold – without my parents even telling me. When I protested, I was told I was too tall for ponies but that I could now have a horse. Despite this silver lining, I was still sad to have lost Rocket. To replace him, Mum had been given an ex-racehorse called It's the Day, and she was the start of what would become a rather expensive habit.

## 2

# So That's What Boys
# are Like

**B**ecause Piers and I were both at boarding school, my parents always made sure we had 'family time' together, so every summer we'd all go on holiday. I always looked forward to our holidays for months ahead and would write about my excitement in my letters to Mum and Dad. They were the only time, apart from Christmas, when we'd all be together.

Of course, all the girls got excited about the summer holidays, especially if their parents lived abroad, as they wouldn't have seen them since the previous year. But, knowing that my house was just seven miles away somehow made it all seem even worse to me. It's hard to take when you know that you've been sent to a boarding school practically round the corner from your home.

Over the past few years, we'd been to Jersey, Turkey and Rhodes, and now we were going to Minorca. I asked Mum

LIMERICK
COUNTY LIBRARY
00504159

if I could have a new swimsuit, so she gave me some money to buy one. Secretly, I bought a gorgeous bright-pink bikini and I was quite shocked to see how womanly my body looked in it in the mirror. I was only 14 but I'd developed quite a decent bust, which seemed to have appeared almost overnight.

Not long before, I'd been one of the last girls at school to need a proper bra. Dad used to joke with me that I needed to do those silly wide-armed stretch-and-release exercises while chanting the mantra 'I must, I must improve my bust.' Then one night, it seemed, it must have worked, because he didn't make those jokes any more. My body was really changing, my hips were curvy and even my face seemed more defined. As I packed my case, ready for a summer adventure, I practised being a Charlie's Angel in the mirror.

We arrived at our hotel, which was lovely, in a place called Binnibecca. I was just getting excited about checking in when I suddenly realised I felt a bit weird about sharing a room with Piers, which was odd, as we'd always shared everything. I think we were both getting to that age when you need a bit of privacy. We knew there was no point in bringing it up on this occasion, as we were already here, but we had a little chat about it and agreed we'd ask for separate rooms next time. We might not have seen eye to eye about everything but we'd always had a good relationship and were still very close. Anyway, Piers was no little boy by now; God knows what he wanted his own room for!

After unpacking, we all went for a walk though the old town. At first, I wasn't aware of it, but I was creating a bit of a stir as we passed among the locals. I was wearing a simple skirt and top, with no make-up, so it wasn't like I was all done up. Once I realised what was happening I was surprised, to say the least. This sort of attention was unknown to me and I wasn't sure if I liked it or not. Dad certainly didn't. He would give the local boys death stares as they tried to catch my eye, and some of these characters were hardly subtle!

As we passed the local bars and headed towards the restaurants, I felt excited and frightened at the same time. Mum, who had her eyes firmly fixed on the craft wares on offer, seemed oblivious. I remember finding it all a bit odd receiving this male attention, especially as some of the men leering at me in the street were older than my father. But, as I'd been at a girls-only school, I was a little curious – certainly not about the old leches but about the ones slightly older than me. Just what were boys really like? A few days into the holiday, I'd get the chance to find out.

I'd been swimming in the hotel pool, which was lovely and had a view of the sea – schoolgirl heaven! – and was just drying myself when out of the corner of my eye I noticed this really handsome guy watching me. I say 'guy' but he didn't look like a man and yet he was no longer a boy. I guessed he was in his mid-twenties and I thought to myself, God, he's gorgeous, he looks like a cross between Lord Byron (minus the club foot!) and Heathcliff (I was reading *Wuthering Heights* at school and had spent many nights in my dark dormitory fantasising about having a Heathcliff all of my own). He was tall, tanned and swarthy with longish dark hair. So good-looking, I thought, but not in a soft way; he seemed to have a rougher edge to him. I managed to get a better look at him as I picked up my towel and headed for the entrance. As I neared him, he smiled. Oh, that's nice, I thought. I like him.

I blushed bright red as I pulled the towel around my new bikini (which had caused Mum's jaw to drop to a new level when she first saw me in it) but I carried on walking towards the hotel, trying my best not to fall over – my feet felt like lead. As I passed him, he smiled again. 'Nice bikini,' he said. Well, I nearly fainted! I managed a meek 'Thanks' and rushed into the hotel lobby, holding the towel around me with a grip one might have used to cling on to the last lifeboat on the *Titanic*. Once in my room, I calmed down a little. I decided that the next time I saw him I must be much more grown up. How embarrassing to go the same colour as the bikini!

The following days passed quite uneventfully, Mum, Dad, Piers and I hanging around the beach, shopping and going for nice meals. And every time I got a Coke at the bar, or just as I was leaving the pool, *he* would suddenly appear and start talking to me, just small talk about nothing really, but it was the most exciting conversation I'd ever had. It was so nice to have someone take an interest in me, especially someone that gorgeous.

A few days before we were due to leave, we were sitting in the bar by the pool when he came in and ordered a drink and waved over at me. 'How do you know him?' Dad asked suspiciously.

'Oh, he swims in the pool when I do,' I replied, as nonchalantly as I could.

Mum, being the kind soul she is, smiled over at him, and before I knew it he was walking over to our table and making small talk with Dad. Piers was nudging me under the table and I wanted the ground to swallow me up before he realised that I was younger than he'd previously assumed. Now he'll know I'm just another little girl on holiday with her parents, I thought.

I was in my own world, worrying about what he must be thinking, when I suddenly realised that I'd heard him introduce himself and then ask my dad if he could take me out for a burger! I looked up at them and then over to Mum. I knew there was no way Dad would let me go off with him, so I thought, if I let Mum know by eye contact that I really wanted to go, maybe she'd understand. I didn't really expect her to do anything, though, as Dad definitely wore the trousers in our house, but this man was so gorgeous it was worth a shot.

Dad was just about to speak when Mum did something I'd never seen her do: she answered for him. 'I'm sure that would be OK as long as you don't go far,' she said and smiled at me. She must have noticed I liked him and decided she would do me a favour, bless her.

I turned to Dad, who was looking in surprise at Mum, and then he said to me, 'Do you want to go, Claire?'

I nodded, not quite believing I was actually being asked.

To my complete surprise, Dad said I could go as long as I didn't go far and was back in two hours.

The man – who I will call Nick – nodded at Dad and smiled at Mum. 'Come on then, Claire,' he said and gestured for me to follow him. I slowly got up from the table, waiting for Dad to suddenly change his mind, and walked over to him. No one stopped me and I carried on walking until we were beyond the hotel gates and out in the freedom of the warm night. I couldn't believe my parents had let me go and I felt a warm rush of affection towards them for trusting me. I wasn't going to let them down.

Nick said he would drive me to a local place he knew, so we headed for his car. As we walked, I decided I wouldn't have any onions on my burger because maybe he might kiss me. I wasn't planning on doing anything else – just a bit of kissing and maybe a cuddle – and then I'd come straight back to the hotel. I wasn't going to be late, as I wanted to prove they were right to trust me.

In hindsight, it sounds awful, doesn't it? Jumping in a car with someone you don't know at 14. In that foreign country this stranger could have taken me anywhere, and my parents just let me go. But such thoughts were far from my mind as we drove down the dusty road. My eyes kept glancing at his mouth, his lips, and I imagined what it might be like to kiss them.

After about ten minutes, we arrived at a bar-restaurant by the sea, where he was very charming and pulled my seat out for me. We ordered some food and talked about ourselves. When I told him about school, he didn't seem surprised, so it appeared he wasn't put off by my age. He chatted about his job at the pool; he had come over from Brighton a few years earlier on holiday and loved it so much he'd decided to stay. I thought it sounded so romantic, a life in the sun with no cares, and, more importantly, no school or parents.

When we'd eaten, he said he wanted to take me to a little bar he liked. 'We can go but not for long,' I told him, as I didn't want to be late. He agreed and we got back in the car. We drove a while and continued chatting. He talked to me as if I was an adult, which I found so refreshing. I wouldn't have had any kind of sophisticated conversation at that age, but I did my best not to sound stupid.

By now, I knew he fancied me, as he kept smiling at me in that way I'd seen on telly. I'd just decided that I definitely wanted to kiss him but, glancing at my watch, I noticed I only had 20 minutes left, so I said we'd have to skip the bar and head back as my dad would be waiting. 'OK,' he said and we drove off. 'See, we're not far,' he said when the hotel was in sight. I smiled, pleased I wasn't going to be late, but then he suddenly turned the car into a side road that seemed to lead behind the hotel.

'What are we doing down here?' I asked when he pulled up at the side of the dark road. 'I just want to talk for a bit, Claire,' he said, as he undid his seatbelt and turned to me.

'I can't. My dad will be waiting for me. Can you turn the car around and drop me at the front, please?' I said, now worried I was going to be late. After all, no one knows where I am and I'm with a man I don't know, I thought to myself.

'No, I want to talk to you. He won't mind if you're half an hour late,' he said, moving closer towards me.

I immediately felt something was wrong. He knew I couldn't be late and here he was telling me I could. 'We *have* been talking,' I said, feeling uncomfortable and with all thought of wanting to kiss him now erased.

He put his hand on my leg and asked me to kiss him. No, I said, because I'd be in trouble if I didn't go back now, and I could always see him tomorrow. Suddenly, his face didn't seem so kind any more and he leaned over and started kissing me. I tried to push him back, saying, 'No, no. I don't want to,' but he ignored my cries and somehow slipped across the seats and was on top of me. He must have put one hand down the side of my seat and pulled the recliner lever, because we were suddenly in the back of the car and completely out of view from the road.

By now, I was really frightened, shouting again at him to get off me. He whispered in my ear in a horrible, strained voice, 'Don't mess me about, you little bitch – you know you want it.'

I was terrified. I didn't actually know what 'it' was but I was beginning to have a pretty good idea and was determined that he wasn't going to get 'it' from me. I kept saying, 'I don't' and 'No, no, no!' but his hands were all over me and he'd pushed my skirt up. I was trying to pull it back down while pushing his hands away and yelling and screaming. By this time, he'd touched me where he shouldn't. I felt sick and was just beginning to think that I could do no more to stop him.

I must have stopped struggling for a moment, and it was then that he started to unbuckle his belt. Just as he did so, I raised my left leg fast and kneed him as hard as I could between the legs. He shouted out as he reeled back in pain, momentarily letting go of me. I knew, if I was going to escape at all, this was my chance. I quickly grabbed the door handle, somehow pushed the door open and my top half fell out.

'Get back here, you fucking tease,' he spat, as he grabbed at my legs, trying to drag me back in.

There was no way I was going to let him do that, not now I was half on the pavement and nearly free. Over and over again, I kicked at him until he loosened his hold on me. I must have hit him hard in the face, because he let go, and I was able to wriggle out on to the street. I'd hit my knee on the floor, cutting it quite badly, but I couldn't feel any pain as I stumbled to my feet and half-ran, half-stumbled back up the side road and towards the hotel.

Too frightened to look behind me, I didn't know if he tried to chase me. I just knew I had to run as fast as I could, so I did. As I came closer to the hotel, still running, I saw Dad pacing up and down outside the main entrance. As he caught sight of me tearing towards him, his face drained of colour. In that spilt second between seeing him and reaching him, I realised that if I told him what had happened to me he'd never let me have my freedom again. And, although tonight had gone horribly wrong, I wasn't going to tell anyone what had really happened and let one man ruin any chance of my having that freedom in the future.

When I reached him, I ran straight into his arms and burst into tears. I'd never been so pleased to see anyone, and Dad, who wasn't normally a tactile man, flung his arms around me as I said, 'Sorry, sorry, sorry.' He looked me straight in the face and asked me if I'd been attacked. I sobbed, 'I haven't,' and told him I was crying because I knew I was late and that I hadn't wanted to let him down after he'd let me go out. I burst into tears again, telling him I loved him.

Dad looked confused and suspicious but I managed to convince him that, realising I was going to be late, I'd made my own way back and got lost, then I'd hurt my knee climbing over a wall after ending up at the back of the hotel. This seemed to calm him and he told me to go to my room and get cleaned up. I ran up the stairs to my room, and luckily Piers wasn't there – he must have been with Mum. I was still crying when I jumped into the shower and started to wash the dirt from my legs and hands. It was at least half an hour before I turned the water off.

Even though I knew I hadn't led Nick on, I accepted that I had to take some responsibility for what had happened. I should have got out of the car when my instincts told me something was wrong. I doubted I could have done anything different, but these things go through your mind. He'd assumed I would do anything he wanted, and probably most of the girls he met on the island were happy to drop their knickers for him – but not me. I knew I'd learned a valuable lesson and I was definitely going to be warier of *all men* from now on.

What shocked me most was how someone could try to exert that sort of control over you. Because he was stronger than me, he'd used that to his advantage, and I've since learned that that's something a man will always have over a woman. Nearly always, anyway. Females, I think, are mentally stronger, and clearly that was how I got over it. But I knew life would never be quite the same again. I'd had a rude awakening, but knew I was lucky as it could have been worse. I never saw him again during the rest of the holiday and we never brought the subject up.

I went back to school feeling I might be best sticking to my horses, and stopped reading *Wuthering Heights*.

# 3

# Hey, Mr DJ

After the 'Minorca incident', I pretty much stayed away from boys until after my sixteenth birthday. This had been made fairly easy by still boarding at an all-girls' school. I wasn't too upset about it, as by then I was involved in the show-jumping and eventing circuit, going to the Ripley and Great Yorkshire shows, which were always full of boys.

At Ripley, one in particular had caught my eye. His name was Robert Smith and he was the son of Harvey Smith, who was famous for sticking two fingers up during a televised show-jumping contest and claiming it was a victory salute! I liked Robert because he would talk *to* me whenever I'd see him, whereas other boys seemed to just talk at you, or your chest, or wouldn't talk to you at all. I used to go to his family's yard for tea and cakes and his mum, Irene, would pick me up and drive me home.

It was all very innocent really. Sex was never on the

agenda (not that I was aware of, anyway), though we used to snog in the haystack, with Robert's younger brother, Stephen, trying to spy on us. We never went any further than first base and it's ironic that our relationship wasn't sexual, as one day, arriving home after having been at Robert's yard, I was called into the sitting room to see 'your father'.

My dad informed me in no uncertain terms that I would be going on the Pill – and there were to be no ifs or buts about it. I protested that we weren't doing anything that warranted this, but there was no arguing with him and the next day he marched me down to our local doctor, who put me on the Pill. It was all very embarrassing, as Dr Crawfurd-Porter had known me since I played with Dinky toys and here he was talking to me about the importance of not getting pregnant.

Even though I was coming up to school-leaving age, I still felt fairly young. *Top of the Pops* was my favourite television show and I just couldn't get enough of music. Most Saturday afternoons I could be found flicking through the Top 40 in WH Smith's record department in Harrogate, where I used to buy loads of singles every week.

The punk scene was slowly filtering into our town and I would see a few 'out there' people dressed like their idols the Sex Pistols or the Clash. Because I was chatty and far from shy, I naturally gravitated towards them, quickly becoming friendly with 'Mad Mary', whose spiky, coloured hair and attempts to win the world record for body piercings done at home were well known throughout the town; Murphy, whose two pet ferrets, Rigor and Mortis, went practically everywhere with him; and Rabbit, a cute-looking punk who lived in Electric Avenue – where the road sign was constantly being stolen, somehow turning up in his bedroom each time!

Since I was now hanging around with people who dressed the way they felt, I started getting more into punk gear myself – much to my parents' disgust! I wasn't trying to make a statement, just to match my appearance to the way I felt inside: a bit different. I didn't fancy tattoos or piercings but I was getting a bit rebellious, the way teenagers do, and decided the time was right to start experimenting with hair colour. I didn't have anything too wild in mind at first; I just wanted to be a bright blonde instead of a dark one.

So one day my friends Rachel Crossley-Smith and Sarah Stewart, who were in my year at school, decided we'd dye one another's hair. We started with mine, and the look on Rachel's face indicated that there was something very wrong with my new bleached mane. Looking in the mirror, I saw that it had come out bright orange. More Bonnie bloody Langford than Debbie Harry! As I set off home, I decided that what everyone said about home-dye kits was true.

When she saw it, Mum was less than pleased and to teach me a lesson said I was not allowed to re-dye it and would have to grow it out. Well, this was bad enough, but, because my hair was naturally a darker shade, as the roots came through I became nicknamed 'Skunk'; it wasn't a very attractive nickname or look. The teachers weren't happy with my new image either, although I was secretly enjoying the attention from my punk mates. I made out that the mishmash of colour was intentional!

So, by accident, the 'skunk look' was my first foray into being a punk. I started hanging round with Mad Mary's gang more and more and when *The Rocky Horror Show* came to the Hyde Park cinema in Leeds we all went along dressed to kill. I loved hanging around with them and felt I'd finally found my little niche. We used to go to punk gigs around Yorkshire, bands like the Undertones, the Ramones and the Clash, and always had a wicked night wherever we were.

My extracurricular look and activities didn't go down too well with our house mistress, Mrs Ireland, who, whenever she saw me, would remark, 'You hardly look like a good advert for Harrogate Ladies' College.' This didn't bother me though, as I was more than ready to leave school and, because I wasn't particularly academic, my parents were happy to let me finish later that year. The only subjects I'd been good at were sport and art. Since I loved animals, I had the idea that I wanted to be a vet, but once I found out that you had to study and pass all the sciences – I particularly hated science – I quickly ditched the idea.

'What *are* you going to do then? Dad kept asking me. When I replied that I still didn't know, he said that I would either have to do a secretarial course, as it was always something I could fall back on – or go back to education. I knew there was no point in arguing with him, as I didn't have a valid reason not to do one or the other, nor did I want to stay on at school, so off to Harrogate College of Further Education to do a secretarial and business course I went.

In order to get to and from the college, I argued, it would be much more productive for me to be on time, and also I wouldn't have to depend on lifts, if I had my own car. (If I had to do this course, at least I wanted to get a bonus out of it.) My parents said they'd help me buy a car once I'd learned to drive. Always up for a challenge, as soon as I turned 17 I took my driving test and passed first time, of which I was rather proud. Dad had bought Piers an old banger to drive round the fields when he was 13, so I'd got quite used to being in a car.

Not long after I passed, Dad bought me my first car, a little blue F-reg Mini 850 that cost £150. It didn't go very fast but I fell in love with it instantly and christened it Howie, after a guy I fancied at college. Howard Smith was really good-looking, six foot tall, with a great body and shiny dark hair, and always wore skin-tight butcher-style strides, which made his bum look great. On the college grapevine, I'd heard he liked me too, so I wanted it to be perfect if we were to go out together. It would be best, I decided, to know what I was doing when I slept with him. All my friends were at it, so I chose another lad I'd recently met as my practice run before the main event. It all sounds absolutely ridiculous now, but as a teenager I thought it seemed like a perfectly reasonable idea.

I'd met Jason Gardiner – I'd just turned 17, he was 18 –

through going out in Harrogate. Two groups of friends had merged and the two of us had sort of clicked, although I wasn't actually going out with him. There'd been some kissing and flirtation but nothing serious until he invited me over to his house for a barbecue one Saturday. I knew that would be the perfect day to execute my plan. Whenever I saw Jason, there were normally about 20 of us, but now it would be just the two of us – plus his family, of course. I'd decided he would be my first, not because he was special, actually more because he wasn't. I suppose I wanted to be in control of the situation and knew I wouldn't be if I was swooning all over someone. So Jason it was to be.

Even though sex was all we'd really talked about at boarding school, I didn't have a clue how I was going to feel, which was just as well really. I'd been at the barbecue for a couple of hours, making small talk with Jason's parents and eating too many sausages, when he asked me if I wanted to have a look at his new video game – in his bedroom. I knew instantly *why* he really wanted to take me to his bedroom. Well, let's just get it out of the way, I thought.

Once we were in his room, Jason was all over me. We'd barely made it on to the bed or got all our clothes off when *it* started happening. The whole thing was rather quick and more than a bit awkward. His elbow was on my hair and he nearly pushed me off the bed at one point! When it was over, he collapsed, momentarily squashing me underneath him, and then rolled over and lit a cigarette – without offering me one.

My overwhelming feeling was, is that all there is to it? Was that it? For a brief moment, I found myself wondering if we'd actually done it at all. Checking my body, I knew we had, but, even though I hadn't known what to expect, I hadn't expected it to be like that.

We only did it once and I think we both used each other as practice runs – I'm pretty sure it was his first time too. If that's what sex is like, why is everyone so desperate to do it? I wondered. I also remember thinking I hadn't bled – at school the rumour was that you might soak the bed with blood – and came to the conclusion I must have broken my hymen through horse riding. Hardly the sort of thought you expect to have straight after your first time. But that is what was running through my mind as I gazed out of the window at the summer sky.

With hindsight, it was all a bit surreal. I felt disappointed that it wasn't the special experience you hope it will be. But it wasn't Jason's fault. I'd made the decision to sleep with someone I wasn't in love with, so I had to take the responsibility. After that, we still saw each other out and about with our mutual friends but we never got together again. There was no heartbreak, because it had been no more than an experiment really.

Being able to drive meant I could get an evening job and continue my pursuit of freedom. I started waitressing in the Damn Yankee, a burger bar that was the new place to be in Harrogate. I used to start my shift about 4.30 in the afternoon and work till about at 1am. It was a bit of a shock to the system at first but I loved the fact that I was earning my own money. My pay, about £7 per shift in the week and £9 per shift at the weekends seemed quite a lot to me at the time. But while it was enough to buy the essentials, I knew the only way to make any decent money was from tips, and that's where I used to really work my magic.

When customers came through the door, I would always walk over and greet them. Some of the other staff seemed to think this was a bit odd, as we didn't have to do it, but by sizing them up in advance I could guide the people I wanted to serve to my table and weed out the others. It was easy to tell who would tip well if you treated them right. For example, a young couple would rarely tip, despite you practically tap dancing for them, so I'd always let them go into someone else's section, but, if it was a rugby team or a family with children, I'd welcome them into mine. You could always make more tips out of those types because there were so many levels on which you could relate to them: flirt with Dad, be matey with Mum, friendly with the kids, while the rugby boys were always putty in my hands.

I knew that I wasn't bad-looking, but I wasn't exactly enhancing my looks with my pink, purple and orange hair and leopard-skin clothes! Some of the customers did give me odd glances to start with but they'd always warmed to me by the time they'd paid the bill. I never really had any grief, because my style wasn't too outrageous. Although I looked fairly punky, it was in a pretty way rather than extreme. I certainly wasn't the safety pins through the nose and bondage gear kind of girl, so at work I managed to surf the fine line between curious and acceptable!

My favourite part of my make-up routine was to spend copious amounts of time getting my eyes just right. I would use lots of Biba make-up, which came in really garish colours and, if applied heavily, was guaranteed to get you noticed. This look wasn't going down too well at the college, but I wasn't bothered what the people there thought of me as I mainly hung around with Clare Pears (also into her horses) and Fiona McKie (from boarding school), who were on my course and also didn't seem to fit in with the rest of the students. At that time, what most girls from Harrogate Ladies' College did after A levels was to go to finishing school, get married, have children and then settle into life as the perfect housewife. I didn't know why, but I just wasn't that way inclined at all.

Leaving school, learning to drive and getting a part-time job had given me a taste of freedom but now I wanted more. It was a strong feeling of wanting to break away from the life that appeared to be set out for me. I couldn't explain how I felt to anyone else or even to myself, but I just felt like I didn't fit in and was quite happy not to. I'd had a brief relationship with Howard, which was sweet, fun and taught me that all the fuss about sex was definitely not unfounded, but I hadn't wanted a serious relationship with a local boy, as I was intent on moving out of my home and getting away. I wanted to earn my *own* money so that I could become even more independent.

After I finished at the college, I managed to last six months at our local estate agents, which I hated, and was still working evenings at the burger bar when Dad asked me to do some secretarial work for him. So now I knew why he'd suggested that course! I started full-time at Dad's office built on the side of our house, which was great as I could have a lie-in. But, although I enjoyed working for Dad, living *and* working at home made me crave a change of atmosphere more than ever.

Luckily, since I was one of the few who had their own car, I was able to escape by driving my mates to sample the thrills of nightlife in Leeds. The place to be at the time was the Warehouse, the busiest club in the city. People would travel from miles around to visit the club, with its great DJs and massive dance floors with ultra-modern lighting.

By now Piers was also well into the punk scene, having made a recent botched attempt to bleach his hair with Domestos and taken to accessorising his outfits with whatever he could lay his hands on. One day he put a padlock and chain of Dad's around his neck and promptly lost the key. Dad was less than impressed when he had to lop the chain off with a bolt-cutter. I topped this with a Mohican which prompted one of the biggest-ever rows with my parents and it was one of the only times Mum and I really fell out. So much for the hairdresser at Vidal Sassoon who assured me they'd love it!

My friends Sarah Baron, from Harrogate, and Fiona were also punks by now – although, because Fiona's parents were strict, she was a closet punk, having to sneak out of her house in 'normal' clothes and change at mine or in the car – and whenever we weren't at the Warehouse we'd go to as many of the gigs we fancied as possible. Fiona and I would take it in turns to drive, which was nice as it meant I didn't always have to be the sober one. Sarah's mum was really sweet and, whenever Sarah and I set off on what she called our 'road trips', she would always fill the car boot with shovels, gloves, flasks and rugs, 'just in case you break down'. We always thought it would be highly embarrassing if anyone ever opened that boot – God knows what they would have imagined we were up to!

After we'd hit Leeds quite a few times, we broadened our horizons and started going to Leicester, Doncaster, Newcastle or anywhere there was a decent band playing. Knowing our parents wouldn't have approved of us driving such long distances, we never told anyone where we were going, which, looking back, was complete madness. Young girls driving all over the country in the dead of night in a clapped-out old mini doesn't bear thinking about these days, but luckily we never found ourselves in any real trouble.

One night, we drove over to Bradford to see the Skids. The lead singer was called Richard Jobson and when I saw him on stage, even though he wasn't the type I usually fancied, I found him strangely attractive. With his blond hair, swept up with a headband, a big chin, baggy trousers and a ripped T-shirt, he certainly stood out from the crowd.

Fiona and I were at the front of the gig when he was on and I seemed to have caught his attention, as he kept singing parts of their songs to me, which was quite erotic.

After the gig, we were invited backstage by a roadie and after a few drinks with the crew I was introduced to Richard, who, to my surprise, was charming, witty *and* intelligent. We hit it off straight away and had loads to talk about, but when he asked us to go back to the hotel for a few drinks I said no. There was no way I was offering myself to anyone on a plate and Fiona and I certainly weren't up for jumping into bed with any muso who invited us, like some of the groupies we used to see at the gigs. We just liked the music, and occasionally the singers. So Richard and I swapped phone numbers and he promised to call me soon. I was pretty sure he would.

A few days later, he rang me at home, asking if I wanted to go and see him at another of their gigs, in Sheffield. I wasn't doing anything special and was fairly intrigued, so I agreed. Mum and Dad had gone away for a few days, leaving just me and Piers at home. I knew I shouldn't, but the opportunity was just too good to miss. I decided to use Mum's new Jeep, which was a horrible pea-green but went faster than mine. Dad had asked me to get some gas canisters filled before they came home, so I thought I'd do that on my way to the concert.

As I was driving over to the yard, a sheep strolled out of nowhere, and not wanting to hit it I swerved hard and went straight off the road and into a tree. Luckily, I wasn't hurt as I had my seatbelt on, which was a rarity in the country, but Mum's new Jeep hadn't fared so well: the front was all smashed up. Shit! I thought. They'll never believe I swerved to miss a sheep. God knows what will happen.

I knew it would be easiest if I just had it fixed before they came home, so I had no choice but to abandon the concert, drive straight over to see my mate Daz, who ran a panel-beating business near by, and beg him to fix it before the next morning. Luckily, Daz owed me a favour and agreed to do it for a 'mate's rate'.

While I was waiting, I called Richard to tell him what had happened and said I wouldn't be able to make it. He asked if he could still come over after the gig since it was so close to me and, although I knew Mum and Dad would have gone mad if they'd known, I really fancied him and thought, Well, if he does stay, I'll have the chance to get up in the morning, get the Jeep and clean up before they get back and Richard leaves. So I agreed.

When Richard arrived late that evening, looking rather yummy, we quickly polished off the two bottles of wine he'd brought with him and before long were committing the cardinal sin of having sex in my parents' bed. It was better than with Jason or Howard and I decided that maybe sex wasn't so bad after all.

The next morning, I woke in a panic, frantically worried that we'd get caught. I told Richard that we'd have to leave at once, as we'd slept in later than I'd planned and I still had to collect the Jeep. I wanted to drop Richard off quickly and then pick up the Jeep before setting off to fetch my parents from the airport. Knowing I wouldn't have enough time to wash and dry their sheets, I'd asked Piers, who had given me cheeky looks about having Richard over, to do it for me. He agreed and I dashed out with Richard, crossing my fingers that the Jeep would be fixed and I'd get away with the past 12 hours' naughtiness. Luckily, when I got to Daz's, the repair looked fine. One down, I thought, as I dropped off Richard and sped off towards the airport.

No one noticed the Jeep's new front and when we got back home everything looked clean and tidy and Mum and Dad seemed pleased. I'd just sighed a secret sigh of relief and was making a cup of tea, when Dad shouted from upstairs, 'Claire, get your arse up here – now.' Straight away, I knew that Piers hadn't made their bed and I was busted. I walked towards their bedroom, knowing there was no excuse that would work. I'd committed what my dad would later call a 'heinous crime' and had been well and truly caught out.

When I entered their room, Mum and Dad were standing staring at the bed, which was still bare. Dad went absolutely mad, calling me all the names under the sun. Mum looked equally angry. I was grounded for two weeks and not even allowed to use the telephone – no mobiles in those days, which made the punishment extra hellish. I knew it was a fair cop, though, so I didn't bother fighting back, but just took it on the chin and decided that now was definitely the time to start looking for a flat of my own before I got myself into any more trouble.

I continued seeing Richard for a while and, one night, when I hadn't seen him for a couple of weeks, he invited me down to stay with him in London. We were having a lovely night in and I was really enjoying being away from home, when we heard the sound of the front door opening and suddenly a blonde girl let herself into the living room and called out Richard's name in a husky voice. Luckily, we were just sitting on the sofa, which was not what we'd been doing an hour before. I knew who she was immediately, as I'd seen her in the papers with some other rock stars: Mariella Frostrup.

She and Richard walked into the kitchen, leaving me feeling very uncomfortable and wondering why on earth he'd invited me down if he was going out with her. He certainly hadn't mentioned her to me. I couldn't fully hear the conversation but about ten minutes later Mariella stormed out of the flat and Richard sat back down, saying nothing about it. I didn't feel able to ask him what was going on – I was only 17 and had never been in a situation like this before.

Richard broke the tension by saying we were going out to meet some mates and said we'd leave once he'd got changed. I nearly died when he came out of his bedroom wearing a Nazi overcoat and matching cap. It wasn't even a fancy-dress party we were going to, although that still would have been no excuse, and I refused to walk beside him in the street. I was a punk, but I thought that was way over the top, even though people wore anything in those days and didn't care about the symbolisation.

Richard was frosty with me on the walk and, when we got to the party, which was for Siouxsie Sioux of the

Banshees, he was still quite off-hand. As this was his circle of friends and I didn't know anyone else, after an hour or so I left – and he didn't even try to stop me! So that was the end of that liaison, but I wasn't heartbroken, as I'd secretly had my eye on someone else. And now I was single again I could do something about it.

# 4

# Sex, Drugs and Rock 'n' Roll

I'd become a regular at the Warehouse in Leeds with Sarah, Fiona and Grace Muddiman, a Goth who'd joined our pack. We practically lived there and I'd recently found myself taking a shine to Marten Reid, the club DJ. I hadn't fancied him when I'd first seen him spinning the decks: he was a bit mad-looking, to say the least, with a shock of blond hair stuck up like a pineapple, and he always wore red plastic pants of the MC Hammer/David Bowie variety, though definitely more MC than DB. But, despite his appearance, after speaking to him several times over as many weeks to request our favourite songs, like the Clash's 'White Riot' and Iggy Pop's 'Loco Mosquito', I soon realised he was really sweet and found myself quietly eyeing him up.

One night in the club, I asked Marten for a song and he said he'd only play it for me if I'd go to the cinema with him in Harrogate. Cheesy! I thought, but the fact that he knew I lived there and was willing to make the effort to come to see me made me feel quite flattered, so I said yes. After the film, we went for dinner and had a really good time. I agreed to see him again and pretty soon we were dating. Whenever I went over to Leeds, I'd stay at Marten's place in Headingley, where he shared the house with his mate Ziggy Monroe, a similar music freak, who always made me feel welcome. I enjoyed staying there but spending time away from Harrogate had made me even more determined to make some major changes in my life. Now I really wanted to rent my own flat and find something more exciting to do for a living than just typing for Dad. So many of the people I knew, including Fiona by now, seemed to be in a band or involved in music in one way or another. Why not give it a try? I thought. I knew I was 'alright' looking and could sing a bit, so there had to be a way to get myself into a band. The only problem was how to tell Dad I wanted to give up my full-time job and move out.

I'd previously been moaning to Sarah about how much I wanted to get my own place. She'd moved out of her parents' home six months previously and this had made me even more impatient. Then one day she told me that Mark Hutchinson, a mutual friend from Harrogate, had mentioned that a room in his shared flat was going and had asked whether I was interested in it, the only catch being that I would need to move in straight away otherwise the landlord would put someone he knew in. At last! Unless it was on fire or under water, I was determined to move in! I knew Mark was all right, as he and his mate Simon Birkhead used to go clubbing with us in Harrogate, and, although it was all a bit quick, I said yes immediately.

The next day, I packed everything I owned into cases and tied them to my roof rack. I knew there was going to be no easy way of announcing my departure, so once I'd finished loading the car I walked into the kitchen, where my parents were sitting, and bit the bullet. 'I'm moving out – right now,' I told them, trying to sound as determined as I could.

Mum looked at me with shock and became really upset, which made me feel awful, but I really needed to get out and quickly was the only way I could think of. Dad just looked at me as though I was joking, until I announced that I'd already packed my car, and then he knew I was serious.

Nervously, they asked me where I was moving to and when I said that the flat was just down the road in Knaresborough and that I'd still be coming back to work for Dad every other day – I would spring my intention to quit the job on them a bit later, I'd wisely decided – they seemed to accept that it could have been worse and waved me off as happily as they could in the circumstances.

I think it wasn't as bad as it could have been because A: they knew I'd be close by and still working at the house most days, so it wasn't like I was heading off to backpack in Outer Mongolia; and B: I'd been away at boarding school for such long periods they'd secretly got quite used to me living away from home. It was probably a bit insensitive to announce I was going just as I was moving my stuff out, but I was 17 and when you make decisions at that age you act on them then and there.

Fiona helped me move into the flat, a three-bedroomed, somewhat grotty affair above George Heapy's record shop in the marketplace in Knaresborough. I didn't care that it wasn't the Ritz, as I finally had my space, although not my peace – Hutch's drum kit was something I hadn't bargained for and it would eventually cause us to be evicted. But, before that happened, Fiona and I made the most of my newfound freedom. She'd come over most nights and we'd punk ourselves up with the hair tongs and start slapping the make-up on. Hutch and my other flat mate, Tony Brooks, used to love seeing our transformation from sweet country girls to rock rebels. Tony was really cool and always up for a laugh and we all got along nicely – if a little noisily!

Another mate of the lads, Simon, lived on our sofa, so in the end there were three blokes and me – it was all strictly platonic, of course. It worked quite well because we were independent and lived our own lives but also had fun whenever we were together. After a while, Marten moved into my room with me, so we were quite a crowded house. It was even more crowded the day Marten decided it was a good idea to buy 500 knocked-off loo rolls and store them in the sitting room in the hope of selling them on. Needless to say, that was the one thing we always had in, as it turned out no one wanted to buy them from him!

Opposite the flat was a really rough club called the

Walleston and our Sunday night's entertainment used to consist of me, the boys and my hairdresser mate Caroline Prince – hairdressers were a punk's best friend – hanging out of the top window winding up the drunks at closing time. We used to get them really annoyed and watch them stumble around shouting. It was a good job we were quite high up, otherwise they'd have come and got us.

While getting ready for a night out, Fiona and I would have a couple 'for the road', Pernod and blackcurrant being our first choice, although we'd settle for whatever we could get our hands on when the Pernod bottle was empty! Once we were ready, we'd pick a gig and set off in the car. Whoever was driving would promise not to get too drunk, but that often changed once we were out and about and in those days it wasn't unusual for us – or many others, for that matter – to drive annihilated.

Coming back from one gig – I can't recall who was driving but we were both absolutely hammered – we were thinking we'd got away with it, when a police car stopped us at a roundabout. We were absolutely terrified as two male officers came up to the window. They asked us if we'd been drinking and we slurred that we were OK to drive and smiled as sweetly as we could, although it was obvious we'd had a good few too many.

Instead of breathalysing us, as we were expecting them to do, they asked us how far we had to go to get home. We said it was only a couple of miles, when in fact we had an hour and a half's journey ahead, so they let us go after warning us it wasn't safe to be out alone and telling us to get home quickly. The police always used to look out for female clubbers out alone at night because that was the time when Peter Sutcliffe, 'the Yorkshire Ripper', was on the loose in the area.

One night, after an evening at the Warehouse, I'd dropped some friends off in the early hours in Headingley, the student area of Leeds, and gone home to sleep. The next morning, I learned from the news that the Ripper had struck just yards from where I'd dropped them off, and just minutes later. It was an awful realisation of just how vulnerable we were – he could have got any of us. After such a close call, whenever I dropped anyone off at night, I always made sure I left them right outside their door.

Since I was nearly always with Marten when he worked at the Warehouse, he let me try my hand on the decks – after I'd asked him about a hundred times! Once I'd got the hang of it, I surprised both of us with how quickly I picked it up and enjoyed it. I'd been getting bored just standing beside him, so, when he'd shown me the ropes and I felt confident enough to be left on my own, I started covering for him while he went to the bar or the loo. And before long I didn't want to let him back on when he returned. The club was owned by a really nice guy called Mike Wyand and his mum, Blanche, a Canadian with a real zest for life. Blanche used to be on the door and take the coats, and was really lovely. She lived in Knaresborough, not far from us, and would often come around for Sunday lunch.

Mike had noticed me on the decks and suggested I do

shifts myself as they'd never had a female DJ before. I liked the idea of being in control of the music and I jumped at the chance. So, every Friday and Saturday, I'd share the night with Marten and it worked really well because we liked different things, so the clubbers got the best of both worlds.

People would come up to you with a request, offering to buy you a drink if you played it, and you became quite well known. While I loved being a DJ, the desire to actually be in a band was still strong and I continued looking out for other possibilities. Through DJ'ing, I met a guy called Stevie Hulme, who was forming a group. Having heard I was looking to be in a band, he asked if I was interested in joining his. Was I ever! He had played in various line-ups over the years, so his latest, To Be Continued, took shape really quickly, and only two weeks after I joined Stevie announced we were going on tour! Marten got really uptight and said if I went we would have to finish. I didn't like that sort of attitude at all, so we soon split up.

Although I loved Marten, it wasn't a life-or-death type of love, so off I went to Amsterdam – me and four blokes in the back of a smelly Ford Transit. My parents weren't too happy, but I was living away from home, independent and very stubborn. Looking back, I suppose I didn't give their reaction too much thought. They knew that, if they had tried to stop me, I'd have gone anyway. That's what you're like when you're young: you do what you want.

The tour was all a bit shambolic but masses of fun. We

covered Iggy Pop and Black Sabbath songs and were truly awful, but the crowds seemed to like us. Mind you, they were mainly stoned or drunk. We toured the Netherlands supporting weird ranting poets, who were big there at the time. As bad as we were, it seemed things were really happening. One minute, I'd been living with my parents and working for Dad, then I'd left home, got a live-in boyfriend and started DJ'ing, and now I was touring abroad as the singer of a rock band. We weren't big league – we weren't even little league – but I really felt like I was living. Also, I started dating Stevie, which worked quite well, as we were constantly together.

After we got back from the tour, I found out that Hutch's late-night drumming, which had caused us many previous complaints from the neighbour, had finally led to our lease being revoked. Not wanting to move home after I'd had a taste of freedom, I accepted when Stevie invited me to move into the house where he lived, in Leicester Grove, Leeds. It seemed like a good idea to be there until I could find a flat of my own, as we were getting on really well.

Leicester Grove was where anybody who was anybody in Leeds lived at that time. The street was scuzzy and full of punks. It was fun for a while, but I knew I could never stay somewhere like that for long. The whole house was gay apart from Stevie and myself. Marc Almond – I knew him from the Warehouse and, although he wasn't that famous yet, he was already pretty cool – lived there and he was quite a laugh, always up to something in the middle of the night, and it wasn't cooking. Annie, who used to play keyboards for Marc's group, Soft Cell, also lived there with her poodle, Pervert.

It was a madhouse. There were screaming catfights, strange one-night-standers roaming the landing (not mine!), rows over who had eaten what, whose knickers were whose and who'd been using whose bed with whom. I was really into Stevie at the time and even loved our mad lifestyle, until one night, on returning from dinner with Mum and Dad, I let myself into the house and went up to our room hoping to surprise him, only to find him in our bed with another girl. I couldn't believe it – I felt like someone had punched me in the stomach.

I screamed at her to get dressed and dragged her out of the bed, telling her to get out. As she sheepishly went down the stairs, I felt a pang of guilt. I couldn't throw another woman into the street at 2am, even though she was in my bed with my boyfriend. So I let her sleep on the couch and then went back to our room, where Stevie was waiting, white as a sheet.

He was clearly scared he was going to get a bollocking, and we did have a massive screaming row – which wasn't like me at all. I told him exactly what I thought of him, that he was 'a cheating scumbag bastard', and that it was over. As I went to pack my things, he begged me not to leave. He kept saying how sorry he was and how he didn't want it to be over. Eventually, he persuaded me that he'd made a mistake and that he wouldn't do it again, and for some reason I found myself getting back into bed with him and agreeing to forgive him.

But, as he lay beside me, my heart was really aching. He'd hurt me badly, yet I didn't want him to see what he'd done to me, so I pretended that everything was OK and fell asleep uncomfortably in his arms. I woke up later that night and couldn't shake the thought from my head that he didn't love me enough, otherwise he wouldn't have slept with her.

After that incident, Stevie made more of an effort to keep our relationship going, and I got another flat in Harrogate and we lived there together. But the magic was gone. We tried our best but he missed his life in Leeds and found Harrogate 'too sophisticated' for him. After a while, I realised I wasn't in love with him any more.

Instead, I was about to fall head over heels for someone who, funnily enough, looked rather like Stevie. He was in a band called the Boomtown Rats and his name was Bob Geldof.

## 5

# Boomtown Rat

As Fiona and I left the Boomtown Rats gig in Manchester, having just met Geldof for the first time, I giggled about what we had done. We hadn't expected to meet them at all, so being invited backstage was a real bonus. We agreed that they seemed like nice lads. I'd spent most of our brief stay chatting to Pete and Simon Crowe, the drummer, about Scottish whisky. One of the jobs I'd done with Dad was to drive him round all the Scottish distilleries, as his company processed the yeast they used. The boys had been impressed by my knowledge of spirits and asked me if I could get any knock-off. Typical!

Fiona had got chatting to Johnny Fingers, the keyboard player, but we'd both really wanted to meet Geldof. There had been quite a bit of eye chemistry between me and him, that was for sure. But, because of all the girls hanging around him, I'd kept well clear. In the car home, we played their album full blast as we sped back.

Pete must have passed on our numbers to Robbie, as a few weeks later he called and invited us to their next gig in Sheffield, saying our names would be on the guest list. I called Fiona and she was so excited she screamed down the phone. The only problem was that in the meantime I'd got back with Stevie, who was now convinced I'd been seeing someone else – which I hadn't – and had become really possessive. He knew I fancied Geldof, because I'd joked that they looked alike (years later, when I showed Bob a picture of Stevie, he said, 'Fuck, that looks like me'), so, when Fiona and I went off to see the band again, I had to pretend we were going to a party. Stevie wasn't daft, though, and said, 'I know where you're going – to see the Rats, and that bloody Geldof, aren't you?'

I just laughed and said he was being silly and went off to meet Fiona. I didn't feel guilty about going, as I hadn't done anything wrong – so far.

Anyway, I wasn't going to cry off just because Stevie was insanely jealous. He should have thought about that before he shagged that girl in our bed. And the Rats were bigger than ever now, thanks to 'Mondays' reaching number one, so there was no way I was going to miss the show.

Because of Stevie's attitude, I'd decided to get ready at Fiona's; I didn't want the hassle of him asking me where I was going again and casting his beady eye over what I was wearing. So, over at her place, we got out our old favourite, Pernod, and got punked up. I was wearing a dress I'd made myself out of pieces of leather that I'd put studs in, and I teamed this up with a leather headband and fishnet tights, then did my usual punk-glam make-up.

Driving to the gig, we attracted equal amounts of admiring and horrified glances on the motorway. After going straight to the stage door, where our names were on the guest list, as promised, we were shown through the crowds, to watch the gig from the front of house. It was excellent.

After the last song, we went for a drink at the bar and then headed backstage. Flashing our AAA ('Access All Areas') passes, we were swiftly waved through. The first person I saw was Geldof. 'Hi, how're you doing?' I said, trying to sound cool.

'Excellent,' he said, his eyes burning into mine. 'What did you think of the show?'

'Great – you played some of my favourite songs,' I said.

He smiled and told me the place was soon going to fill up and as we hadn't had a chance to talk last time – ahh, he'd remembered me! – I should follow them back to the hotel and have a proper drink. I wasn't quite sure what to make of this invitation, but Fiona fancied going, so we decided we'd follow them but, if it was like last time, with loads of girls arriving, we'd leave again. And if not, well, who knows? The hotel was near by, so at least we wouldn't have far to go.

After finishing our drinks, we followed the tour bus in Fiona's blue Vauxhall Viva, which she'd named Brian – God knows why – and parked. The hotel was packed as we fought our way up to its club, which was weirdly done out like the inside of an aeroplane. After being there about five minutes, we decided the atmosphere was so good that we wanted to stay as late as possible, but not wanting to have to depend on someone's bed, or to sleep in the car, we went down to the reception to see if we could get a room. Fiona and I would always get a room together if we wanted to stay somewhere extra late. With the Yorkshire Ripper still about and 'Brian' occasionally playing up, we certainly didn't like the idea of being stranded at 4am. If we had a room, we were safe and didn't have to worry about drink-driving.

Unfortunately, when we were told the price it became clear that there was no way we could afford to stay – not on what we earned. Trying not to look shocked, we made our way back up to the club, agreeing we'd play the night by ear and if one of us wanted to leave we'd let the other one know.

I was just leaning over the bar to order some drinks when two strong hands slipped around my waist and a sexy Irish voice whispered in my ear, 'Glad you could make it.'

I knew instantly it was Geldof – at least I bloody hoped it was! – and, acting cool, I didn't turn round until I'd passed Fiona her drink. 'Oh, hello,' I said coolly.

Geldof smiled, clearly amused that I wasn't swooning at his feet. Well, not visibly anyway. I looked at him, not quite believing that here I was with his arms around me in a nightclub. He took us over to join the others, a mix of the crew and band, including Johnny, Pete and the lighting guy, who was always known as 'Super Mick'. Fiona seemed to be getting on really well with Super Mick and everyone seemed to be gelling; mind you, after several drinks people normally do.

Geldof, who was sitting next to me, leaned over and asked if I wanted to go and have a drink in his room. Since we were sitting in front of a table full of booze, I knew he had something else in mind. Grabbing his whisky and dry soda and my vodka and orange, he gestured for me to leave with him. Not quite believing what was happening, I looked over to Fiona, who was watching. 'Go for it,' she mouthed, and before I knew what was happening I was out of my seat as he took me by the arm and led me away from the party. I seemed to be in a trance of desire. I had an overwhelming urge to be with him – something I'd never felt so strongly before. I felt mesmerised.

We'd almost reached the lobby when I suddenly remembered my handbag was on the bar, and as I turned round and reached over to grab it, I knocked two glasses over. I was mortified. 'I can see you're going to be trouble, Claire,' Geldof said and smiled, probably thinking I was drunk, whereas I was just incredibly nervous. I gave a fake laugh as we carried on into the hall. My heart was beating even faster as he led me into a packed lift and we rode up to his floor. People around us were acting normally but I was thinking, Oh my God! I'm about to have sex with someone I really, really want.

We barely talked as we walked up the corridor hand in hand. Once inside his room, I was so nervous I tripped over the carpet runner and fell on to the bed, knocking a table over in the process. He just stood and stared at me with those amazing eyes as I lay there trying to look alluring. It must have worked, because he slammed the door shut, and as he approached me my mind was racing with guilty thoughts. This might just be a one-off and I shouldn't really do it, I was thinking – but I wanted him so badly.

Before I knew it, he'd kicked off his boots and was kissing me on the bed. His kisses were wild and deep and I thought my heart was going to leap out of my throat. Oh my God, I thought, he's so nice. He is just so sexy. He pulled me up off the bed, stood me against the wall and stripped me naked, but he didn't take all his clothes off. In the furious haste of it all, I think he kept his vest or T-shirt on. I was still quite inexperienced sexually but he knew exactly what he was doing and was clearly very experienced. He was well built and would certainly not have had any embarrassment in the changing rooms.

The next three hours in that hotel room were filled with pure, unadulterated sex and lust. He was quite forceful and took full control. He was a lot older than me – I was 17, he was in his late twenties – but when he kissed me he was gentle and tender, taking me to places I'd never been but where suddenly I wanted to go with him. Even though I'd had a couple of boyfriends before (and was sort of back with Stevie at the time), sex with Geldof surpassed anything I'd previously experienced. He knew just what to do with his body to make mine come alive. He knew which buttons to push; the way he made me feel was amazing and he also introduced me to several things I'd never even heard of – which I won't repeat on these pages – but nothing illegal! Not in the UK anyway.

Eventually, we fell asleep but not long after we'd nodded off the phone rang. I answered it, as it was on my side; it was Super Mick, letting me know that Fiona was with him in his room. I was relieved she was OK – this was the first time we'd separated on a night out – but I knew she understood, and by the giggling in the background I could tell she was having a good time herself.

I went back to sleep in Geldof's arms and when we woke in the morning we had sex again, this time more of a quickie but still amazing, and then lay in bed talking. He asked all about me and I told him about my family and the band I was in. He seemed genuinely interested but didn't really talk about himself. But then he didn't strike me as a morning person.

It was eight o'clock and I wanted to check Fiona was OK, so I left him in bed, after kissing him goodbye and saying I hoped I'd see him again soon. I didn't say when or where; it was very casual but, far from upsetting me, it seemed just right. After all, as far as I knew, this might have just been one perfect night. I hoped it was to be repeated but I was prepared to say to myself, well, if he calls, he calls. I'm a firm believer in fate and at that very moment I was more worried about meeting up with Fiona and getting to work. I stumbled along the corridor on cloud nine, looking for her room. Twice I walked past the number Super Mick had told me. I just couldn't think straight.

When I knocked on the door, Fiona answered, made-up and ready to leave. We said our goodbyes and set off down the corridor. We cringed as we made our way out of the hotel in the same clothes we'd arrived in the night before. Walking towards the car, we joked that we were groupies, then reassured ourselves that we weren't, as we'd been *invited* to see the boys and hadn't chased them *and* we hadn't done anything the first time we'd met them. *So,* in our books, although we hadn't exactly behaved like 'Harrogate ladies', we weren't tarts either.

On reaching the car, we saw the front passenger window had been smashed, which upset Fiona, though I was more interested in talking about what had happened the night before. She told me she'd had a really good time until Super Mick had rolled over in the middle of the night and accidentally knocked her out of bed! We compared notes and joked about our 'bedroom activities', the way young girls do, but, while I was laughing about what we'd done, I knew I was in big trouble. Even though I knew it couldn't be real, since I might never see him again, I had a sneaking feeling that I was falling for Bob Geldof, and the thought that he might never call me again made me feel sick.

# 6

# Amsterdam Bound

It was nearly a year before I got the call to go and meet Geldof. Meanwhile, I'd noticed in the papers that he had been 'seeing' the journalist Paula Yates. I only knew who she was because of the book she'd written, *Rock Stars in Their Underpants*, which featured the Boomtown Rats, Bowie, the Stones and even my old beau Richard Jobson. A friend showed it to me. Stevie and I were still technically together, sharing my flat in Harrogate, but we weren't getting on and were arguing more than ever. As it happened, I couldn't go and see Geldof anyway, as we were about to go on tour again ourselves.

Being in the band together hadn't helped Steve and I, and we were not really getting anywhere, either as a couple or in the music industry. I'd made excuses to myself to stay in the relationship, hoping that maybe we could make it work, as we'd been together nearly three years by then. But then one night, at a party to celebrate my brother's birthday, I couldn't kid myself any longer that we had a future.

Piers had decided to give the party a *Mad Max* theme, as the movie was huge then. I'd taken Stevie along, even though we'd been arguing all day because he wouldn't wear a costume, which seemed daft, as he'd lived in leathers nearly every day of his life. One of the main problems was that he was still so Leeds-orientated that he'd never really made many friends in our area, so he only knew a few people at the party, and this seemed to make his mood even blacker.

After several of his snide comments that evening, I'd had enough and said that if he didn't snap out of it he should just bloody leave. This started a massive argument, with the two of us throwing everything we could at each other: drinks, food, furniture and words – he using my supposed interest in Geldof, me using the girl I'd caught him with in our bed. Not wanting to ruin Piers's party and knowing it was getting really nasty, I tried to get Stevie outside to calm down but he stormed off, saying he was going home and I could just 'fuck off'. I shouted after him that it was too far (seven miles) but he just took off, shouting, 'You'd better come back soon or else.' No way, mate, I thought, as I watched him go. He'd wanted a fight all day and now he'd got one, so I was in no rush to go home and get involved in round two.

After a few more hours at the party, and having apologised profusely to Piers for what had happened, I went round to a mate's house who was also having a party and stayed the night there.

Little did I know – and I don't think I would have cared anyway – that Stevie hadn't taken his keys, so he had sat outside the flat for hours and hours waiting for me. Since he hadn't made any mates locally, he couldn't stay with anyone. Eventually, he got into the main entrance of the flats and slept on the staircase. As soon as I arrived home in the morning and let him in, he started shouting that his mum and her boyfriend were coming round for Sunday lunch and because I'd only just got home we wouldn't be able to sort it out in time. Too tired to argue, I said it wasn't too late and started looking through the fridge. I didn't see why they should suffer, as it wasn't their fault.

I was about to suggest a truce when he started accusing me of having slept with someone the previous night. I told him not to be silly and that I'd just been at my mate's house and had crashed out, very much alone, on her old sofa, but he wasn't having any of it. In the midst of this, his mum rang to say they were on their way and he still let them come. I couldn't believe it. But, not wanting to upset his mum, who was a lovely woman, I got on with lunch, knowing that the moment they left I would kick him out.

His mother and her boyfriend arrived and we had a fake-happy lunch. I gritted my teeth as she joked that she'd be buying a hat soon. Ha! No way! After lunch and a few drinks, we drove them to the station, and soon after we'd waved them off the shit really hit the fan. Stevie, who had been so polite during the meal that I'd almost forgiven him, spun round as the train disappeared. I went to put my arms around him but he pushed me away, his arm catching my face and humiliating me in front of all the people on the packed platform. I was shocked. I looked at him in disbelief as he walked off, leaving me standing on the empty platform, holding my face. The anger rose in me immediately. No man treats me like that.

We'd come in my car, and I had the keys, so I drove off to see my mate Jim, who was DJ'ing at the Phono-graphique, a tiny gay nightclub in the Merrion Centre in Leeds. As soon as I arrived, Jim noticed that I looked quite upset. I was just telling Jim what had happened when Stevie walked in and rushed straight over to me. I looked at his face, which I'd grown to detest, and then punched him as hard as I could – right on the nose. It definitely wasn't a girly slap. A belt, I think is the word. And down he went – out cold. I stepped over him and left, shouting that I was putting his stuff in the garden and that we were over for good.

A few days later, he moved the rest of his things out and went back to Leeds. I would never have seen him again if it hadn't been for the fact that we were still both in the band. To Be Continued had previously booked another tour to Amsterdam, which I'd agreed to, and I felt I couldn't let the other boys down, as they'd always been good to me. So a week later I had to set off in the van with all of them, including Stevie.

Each night, we supported one weird band after another, and if it wasn't a band it was some mad poet, like the last time. It was a total nightmare. Hotels that were supposed to have been organised for us said they hadn't been booked when we turned up, so we often had to sleep in the back of the van – all seven of us! Now, our van wasn't very hygienic with six blokes in it every day, let alone when we were sleeping and eating in it too, and no money for B&Bs meant no baths, which was difficult for me, as I just wasn't used to living like that. But, as 'one of the boys', you just had to get on with it.

Stevie had said barely a word to me during the tour but, because of the close-quarters living, we slowly got back on speaking terms and became sort of friends again, though neither of us had any intention of getting back together. One night, we were playing the notorious Milky Way bar in the heart of Amsterdam. The club was really cool, with a backroom that contained a wall of jars that looked like a Woolworths Pick 'n' Mix counter. You could have whatever you wanted to smoke. I was really surprised to see that the clientele was so diverse: a weird blend of long-haired hippies, tie-dyed students, travellers, punks and businessmen.

After each picking our smoke – I chose grass – we set about 'skinning up'. Some of the boys were more experienced than I was at rolling a joint and laughed at mine, saying it resembled something from a *Blue Peter* Christmas special. I knew that dope made everyone feel different, but it just made me laugh and laugh until tears rolled down my face. Then I got a massive attack of 'the munchies' and ate my way through two pizzas and a chocolate cake. I never ate desserts, so I knew I was off my face.

Later, we set off on a tour of the red-light district. The place was packed with drunken men wandering around the huge variety of sex shows and we found ourselves on the street where the girls display themselves in all their finery behind big 'shop' windows. Some of them looked very exotic in their glass booths and they all waved at the boys – and occasionally at me! One strong-looking black girl seemed to have caught the eye of Shep, our driver-roadie, and beckoned him inside. With us all egging him on, he swaggered in, only to run out screaming moments later that she was a he! And he told us all to run. S/he started banging on the window and shouting at us, so we all legged it down the cobbled street before we got into any more trouble.

I found it really strange that you could smoke dope in the cafés or even in the street without getting arrested. One afternoon, after a major smoking session, everyone fancied getting a tattoo. I said I would have a little one done on my ankle but I'd go last. I sat by them as each lad had his done and then at the very last minute I jumped up and ran off laughing, saying I was never going to have that done to me. And I was so glad I did when I saw the mess the tattooist had made of the boys. Maybe they shouldn't have offered him that spliff after all!

Even though we were having a laugh, by now I'd had enough and wanted to go home. I was wondering how I could get off the tour as we were driving back from a gig, when Shep suddenly lost control of the van and we crashed into a bridge, then plummeted down the embankment. I was certain we were going into the water and were about to drown. We were all screaming as the van came to a thunderous halt. After checking that everyone, including myself, was OK, I thought, God, I've got to get away. I don't want to die in a stinking van in an Amsterdam canal. We crawled out of the back of the van, which was badly damaged at the front, and saw we had missed plunging into the water by about three feet. We'd been lucky to get out alive.

With our transport wrecked, that was the end of our trip, so we went home. The tour had been a disaster professionally and it was clear that the band was finished. On our last night together, we decided to call it a day. We'd given it our best shot but we all knew that To Be Continued had just been discontinued. Stevie and I were finished too; although we were talking now, there was no chance of a reconciliation.

Back home again, I was single and directionless. I was sitting in my new living room – I'd moved into a house in Harrogate – with a large glass of red wine one evening, wondering what to do with myself, when Fiona rang asking if I'd like to see Duran Duran in Manchester the following Friday. As I hadn't met up with her in ages and quite fancied the idea of seeing the band, I agreed, and just before the show we booked a hotel near the venue and got ready for a girls' night out. The gig was fantastic and afterwards we headed back to the hotel, as it had a late bar, to catch up with each other's news.

After a few drinks, we became aware that lots of people in the bar were acting strangely, whispering and pointing at the lobby, which was behind us. Turning round, I saw cameras flashing and people pushing and shoving as the boys from Duran Duran made their way into the hotel.

'Oh my God!' said Fiona. 'They must be staying here too!' They were still quite new but definitely hot. I was intrigued by the boys' attitudes and good looks, but, even though I was quite impressed when I saw them, I'm the type of person who prefers to play it cool.

As we looked on, they entered the bar and sat down at a large table opposite us. Simon Le Bon, Nick Rhodes and John Taylor seemed to love the attention, while Andy and Roger Taylor chatted quietly in the corner. Simon, who hadn't taken his eyes off us since arriving, gestured for us to join them for a drink. Fiona was off her seat before he'd said a word and we sat with them for a few glasses of champagne, Simon doing his best to chat me up and John entertaining Fiona. We were having a really good time but I was becoming aware that the lads seemed to be taking us as a sure bet – I'd noticed some eye contact between them – so I suggested to Fiona that it was time we made a move. The boys tried to get us to stay but we thanked them for the drinks and said goodnight.

As we walked along the corridor, Fiona said that she too had noticed the nudge-nudge, wink-winking that was going on and had been happy to leave when we did.

Just as we got to our room, someone called my name out loudly. I turned round to see Simon Le Bon running down the corridor with a bottle of champagne in his hand. 'Don't go to bed yet, Claire – I want to talk to you,' he said.

I was totally surprised by this, and as he reached me he held out the bottle and said, 'At least let's finish this together', gesturing towards my room.

I looked at Fiona, who nodded that we should invite him in, and we then spent the next half-hour sitting on the bed – as Simon tried every which way to get Fiona to go back down to the bar, so that we could be alone. I was really tempted, as he was gorgeous, but I wasn't in the right frame of mind for what looked like it could turn out to be a one-night stand. So, after we'd finished the bottle, I went to the loo while Fiona got rid of him. Ten out of ten for trying, though, Simon!

Some weeks later, I noticed that the Rats were on tour again. Fiona called to say she'd bought us tickets and was coming to pick me up. I'd changed my phone number since I'd last heard from Geldof, so I wasn't sure if he'd tried to invite me, but, always a believer in fate, I took this as the sign I was hoping for. Besides, I thought, what's the worst thing that could happen? I wasn't under any illusion that he'd be waiting for me with open arms, but since I was only 20 I knew I shouldn't be just sitting at home alone, but be out there doing something exciting – and a Rats concert was just the distraction I needed. If I saw Geldof afterwards, that would be a bonus. If not, it wouldn't be the end of the world.

Fiona picked me up on the night of the gig and we caught up on all that had been happening: the disastrous tour, Fiona's new flat and her new job at a graphic design studio – she always was a great artist.

Later, at the venue, I stood a little farther back than the last few times, as I felt a mix of excitement and nerves, just in case he didn't remember me. During the gig, Geldof saw me and smiled. I smiled back and instantly felt a whole lot better.

After the show, some of the boys came out and invited us backstage. As we entered the back bar, Geldof, who was sitting in a corner, looked straight at me with an expression of slight discomfort. I was confused – until I took in the full view. Seated right beside him was a very blonde Paula Yates. I knew from the papers they'd been linked, but I didn't know if they were actually going out or if it was serious. I decided it was probably best not to go over and just smiled at Bob as I passed him on my way to the bar. Paula shot me a territorial glance but I gave her a blank look back. I didn't know her, so I had nothing to apologise for.

After a quick drink with Fiona, I started to make my excuses, ready to leave. Geldof noticed and gave me an apologetic shrug, which I took to mean that he was sorry we hadn't talked, but there was no way I was going to go over and speak with him while Paula was there. I was on my way down the stairs when one of the roadies said that, if I was leaving because of her, I shouldn't. I asked him what he meant and he said that she 'hounded him into being with her', but I was pretty sure Geldof did what he wanted, so I wasn't necessarily ready to believe that.

The roadie said that the rest of the band couldn't stand her and wanted me to stay. He asked for my new number so that he could pass it on to Geldof. It was sweet of him to try to make me feel better but I knew three was a crowd and said I'd see him next time. I gave him my number and was just near the bottom of the stairs when I bumped into Pete. He looked flustered and instead of saying 'Hello', he blurted out, 'Bob's missus is here.' He must have thought I hadn't been to the backstage bar yet. 'So it's probably not the best time to see him tonight, Claire,' he added. I didn't let on that I knew what he was talking about and walked off.

I guess Pete just didn't want the boat rocked, which was fair enough. I'd told Fiona I wanted to leave and she'd been at the bottom of the stairs waiting for me. She could see I was unhappy and we left immediately. We didn't talk about it in the car, as I was too upset about everything that had happened recently.

All thoughts of ever being with Geldof again left my mind and I decided I would put it behind me and move on. I didn't want to chase someone who didn't want me. So, if he didn't contact me again, that was definitely that.

# 7

## Skin on Skin

The roadie must have done as he'd promised, because the morning after the concert I was in bed when the phone rang; I recognised Geldof's voice immediately.

'Why don't you come and see me at one of the northern gigs, where it will be quieter?' he asked.

So I *wasn't* chasing someone who didn't want me after all, I thought, as I wrapped the cord round my fingers and slipped back under the covers.

After a brief conversation in which neither of us mentioned the night before, I agreed that I would come and see him again, at a venue that was close to me, if he thought it was 'appropriate'. What I was trying to ask was whether his relationship with Paula was serious. If it was, I wouldn't be coming. He knew what I was hinting at and somehow talked around the 'issue' while letting me know that he wanted to see me and that there was no reason we shouldn't meet up. Basically, he was saying that our night together wasn't a one-off and that he would like to see me again. I decided that since he'd gone to the effort of calling me, I would go. Besides, I thought, I've made it clear that I don't want to step on other girls' toes – and here he was saying I wouldn't be doing that. So we agreed that I'd see him in a few weeks, when he knew he was fairly near by, and that he'd ring me closer to the time.

Some weeks later, Geldof called and invited me to the gig at St George's Hall in Bradford, which was on the following night. 'Give a girl some notice, why don't you!' I said as I wrote down the details.

'You'll be there,' he laughed, then rang off.

I thought about the fact that he was supposed to be seeing Paula, but everyone, including him, seemed to be saying that she was the 'chaser' in the relationship. And it's not like they're even engaged, I told myself, as I cast an eye over my wardrobe, trying to decide what to wear. So there's no reason I can't go, I decided, picking out a pair of boots with killer heels. And, since Geldof had invited me himself, I knew there was little chance she'd be there. This will be it, I thought. You might still be in with a chance to go out with him. He must like you, otherwise he wouldn't want you there. Be nice, catch up, relax and chill with him. You never know, he might ask you out properly.

The next night, however, my mind was buzzing with all the barriers I was trying to put up in case everything went wrong. As I drove over to the gig I decided that, if I walked in and Paula *was* there, I would just walk away for good –

and, if she wasn't, well, who knows. I arrived after the gig had finished and my outfit caused a bit of a stir among some of the lads I passed. I was wearing a fluffy tiger-skin dress I'd made, fishnets, boots and chains with a choker necklace made of fake barbed wire. I cringe now to think about it, but I felt pretty sexy at the time! I laughed off the comments and wolf-whistles as I made my way towards the backstage entrance.

As I'd walked from the car, I'd given myself another rule. I decided that if my name wasn't on the list at the door I'd just walk away and ignore his calls. But it was, so in I went. Geldof had put me down as 'Speed', his nickname for me, a take on my family name of Seed. I went backstage and into the main room, where he was sitting by the bar. He got up immediately to greet me and said we should go somewhere more private. As the band's hotel was near by, we should go there for a drink, he suggested.

I cheekily shouted to the boys that we were going to the hotel bar, as I didn't want to appear so available, and invited them to join us. Bob laughed and beckoned them to follow. We walked the couple of streets or so to the hotel, Bob and I hand in hand and the others following. The comedian Russ Abbot, who was riding high at the time, was in the bar that night, which seemed to take the heat off Geldof and the boys, so we were pretty much left alone. It suddenly felt quite surreal – here I was, a 20-year-old Harrogate 'lady' sandwiched between these two famous extreme characters!

We sat at a table chatting, Bob drinking just the odd

whisky and dry – I'd noticed by now that he wasn't a big drinker – while I was on my second vodka and orange. I'd found that combination was a good drink for me, as it didn't get me *too* annihilated and I could keep up with the boys, who really knocked back their drinks.

After half an hour or so, Bob whispered to me, 'Shall we go?' I nodded and we went up to his hotel room and immediately to bed. This time it was tender and slow, more exploratory, more intimate, less frenzied, but just as erotic. And we talked about everything – well, *nearly* everything.

He said he wanted to know how my family was and asked me about my background and told me about his. Again, it all seemed unbelievable: 'I Don't Like Mondays' had topped the singles chart and made him really famous by now and here he was telling me his family secrets alone in his hotel room, where everything felt so nice, so special, so us. Later, we slept in each other's arms all night.

In the morning, as I dressed to leave, I said, 'When am I going to see you again?' I had promised myself I would play it cool and not ask the dreaded question, but I was hooked and just couldn't keep it in. As I blushed, he smiled and said, 'I'll call as soon as I'm near you – I promise.'

I felt a mix of elation and worry, thinking, Yes! I'm finally getting somewhere! I'm meaning something to him; it might not be love yet, and he hasn't invited me to London, so I know it isn't the perfect answer, but he's showing me that he cares. I nodded as he kissed me goodbye. And then I set off for work. I was working for my dad again and I was going to be late and very inappropriately dressed! I left the hotel feeling amazing but looking awful.

When I eventually turned up, Dad smiled and asked me what I'd been up to the night before. He knew about me and Bob and just laughed when I told the censored version. I knew there was still a chance I might not hear from Bob again, but over the next few weeks I was busy moving house (again!) so I didn't have much chance to worry whether the phone would ring or not. But, just in case, I'd called and left the new number.

After Stevie and I split, I'd moved into my own house, in Mayfield Grove in Harrogate, for which I paid £16,000. I was painting the living room one day when the phone rang. It was Geldof.

'I'm in Loughborough. Now that's got to be somewhere near you.'

I laughed. 'No – that's in the bloody Midlands!' I said, wiping the paint from my face.

'Oh, come on, Speed, drive over and get me,' he said.

'Tonight! You love not giving me any warning, don't you?' I laughed, before agreeing to drive over and get him. I rushed upstairs and washed the paint from my hair, then got changed.

As I started the car, I noticed I was nearly out of petrol. God, I'll never make it, I thought. I checked my purse – empty. That day I'd bought lots of things for the house and had no cash left. What a night to call, I thought, as I drove over to the Damn Yankee, where I used to work, desperately hoping that the car, which Dad kept telling me was on its last legs, would make it there, and that the restaurant would cash me a £50 cheque. I made it and they did, so I set off for Loughborough. Since it was a two-hour drive, I knew I'd miss the gig and I also knew that, as I was working the next day and the new house was a tip, I really shouldn't be on my way to see him, but I couldn't resist it.

I got to the hotel and went directly up to his room – where he was waiting – and again we went straight to bed. After we'd made love, we talked all night about where our lives seemed to be going. I was disillusioned with my lack of career direction. He was reading a book by Hemingway and suggested some analogies from that, saying that everything happened for a reason.

That night he talked about Paula properly for the first time. I tried to keep calm as I asked how things were going, hoping he was going to tell me it was over and that I was the one he really wanted. 'She's not independent like you,' he said. That sounded like a bit of a brush-off to me, as she was well known by this time for pursuing her own career. Hearing those words, I instantly knew that he was *not* going to finish with her for me – and my heart sank. I started thinking, I really shouldn't be here, I shouldn't have come, and I wanted to leave, as I could feel tears welling up in my eyes.

He seemed to sense this and put his hand on mine and told me that he wanted me to know how special I was to him. I turned to him and said, 'But am I special enough, though? Who do you want to be with, Geldof? Because you can't have us both.'

84

Looking me right in the eyes, he said, 'Look, Claire, I can't live without you – but I can't live with you. Listen to the album *V Deep*. I've written a song for you on it called "Skin on Skin" – that's about you. I do care about you… but you know it's just difficult.' He looked away, and suddenly I thought, OK, that's it, it's over but at least I know he cares. I've said my piece and he's said his, there's nothing left to say.

I packed my bag, put my coat on and walked to the door, neither of us saying we'd see each other again or speak on the phone. I didn't even kiss him goodbye, just smiled at him from the doorway. On the way out of the hotel, I told myself I'd made my peace with what had happened and that I'd have to try to put him to the back of my mind. As I drove home, I played the cassette of *V Deep*, curious to listen to the words of 'Skin on Skin'.

The lyric of the song is pretty sexual and describes the couple's desire for each other but refers to them not wanting to involve themselves in what is right or wrong. The words he had written alluded to a girlfriend questioning the direction of her relationship with her man. What was between them was more sexual than sensual, rather than being about right and wrong. As I listened to the song, I thought about him and that he must love me in his own way.

Some time later, I read in the paper that Paula was pregnant. No going back now, I thought, and with a heavy heart I set about throwing myself into my work and finishing the house. Many months passed quite uneventfully in this way, along with seeing the occasional local boy. Then I noticed in the papers that Paula had given birth to a baby girl, named Fifi Trixibelle, and I even managed to feel genuinely happy for him.

One night I was in my bedroom when the phone rang – it was Geldof. 'Hi, it's me,' he said. I was quite taken aback but played it cool, asking, 'Me who?' He knew I knew it was him and laughed. He said he was going to be in Manchester, at the Midland Hotel, the following night and he needed to see me. Could I go and meet him? He said nothing of the fact that he was now a father and obviously very much with Paula. I knew I should have said no, and I'd run it through my head dozens of times that, if he did call, I would say I was busy or ignore him, but I somehow found myself writing down the address and agreed to see him.

After putting the phone down, I ran myself a bath and lay in it until the water went cold and my young skin prune-like. Should I go or not? I asked myself over and over again – but I knew that I would. I was drawn to him like the proverbial moth to the flame, and I had a suspicion that, if anyone was going to get burned, it would probably be me, but when you're 21 your heart rules, not your head.

The next day went by as if I was on autopilot. I dressed and undressed several times and, having set out, even turned back twice. But, sure enough, that evening I pulled up outside the Midland Hotel and was soon in the lift making my way to the room Bob said he'd be in. I knocked at the door and he opened it, dressed. 'Fancy some food?' he said, closing the door behind him and guiding me towards the lift. 'OK,' I said, quite shocked that he was taking me away from the privacy of his room. He was really famous by now and everyone knew about him and Paula and the baby, so why on earth was he taking me downstairs to the restaurant, where we would be seen together?

People stared at us as we were shown to a table by the bar. He seemed unfazed. Why was he tempting fate? Did he *want* us to get caught? Why was he doing this now? Why hadn't he done it before? All these thoughts raced through my head as we took our seats in the packed restaurant.

While we were eating, I didn't know what to think – and I wasn't confident enough to ask him what he was thinking. Was he trying to say this was cool, that he wanted people to know about us? Was their relationship not as rosy as the papers had made out? As far as political issues are concerned, Bob is very good at getting his point across, but on an emotional/personal level he really seemed to struggle – at least with me. I was quite distant throughout dinner; in my mind, I was trying to break away, as I knew I shouldn't be here and wasn't even sure what we were doing. Yes, I wanted to be with him, but I wanted to be in Paula's position, which was obviously a role that had been filled. Was I now being offered the runner-up role of 'Bob's bit on the road'?

It seemed from the very fact that we were sitting here that I was, but I wanted more than this. I wanted my own boyfriend – not someone else's. After dinner, we went up to his room and, despite my plan to leave, I ended up spending the night. As always, the sex was amazing, if a little rougher than usual. But in the morning I was in such a rush to leave, because I felt guilty, that I left my favourite silver bangles in his room. He called me later to say he'd left them at the reception, but I couldn't face going back for them and told myself I would not be going back to him again either.

A year or so passed – it was now early 1984 – and I was still in Harrogate but really feeling ready for a change of scenery. I'd ignored the occasional invitation to go and see Geldof on tour. I just didn't want to spend my time sneaking in and out of hotels with someone else's boyfriend – even though I did miss him. The band toured every 12 months, so I suppose that was how our relationship had managed to spread over several years yet be based on small amounts of time together.

Still interested in music, I'd started managing a little band called Under the Arch in Harrogate. The only problem was that a limited budget meant they had to rehearse in an old barn their parents owned which was full of bats that attacked you whenever you played too loud – maybe they were trying to tell us something. My friend Caroline Prince and her mate Des Roche, both hairdressers, were planning to put on a charity fashion show for the children starving in Ethiopia, whose plight wasn't well publicised at the time. I suggested the band perform and that we have a hair and fashion show in a local hotspot, Annabella's.

As well as help organise the event, Under the Arch played, and I appeared in the fashion show with my friend Mark Baker, all punked up with horrible black and white nylon hair extensions, with me dressed in a ball gown and him in a suit. We seemed to go down well with the audience as we performed a mock punk wedding and, with the pictures making all the local papers, I had a taste of my own image being out there at last.

The show raised quite a lot of money for the cause, so I was really happy I'd taken part. Late that night, my phone rang, and it was Geldof. After a quick catch-up, I told him about the charity event. He said he knew about the Ethiopian famine following the Michael Buerk report and that Paula had put a picture on the fridge and had been telling him to 'do something for Ethiopia'. I told him how the people seemed to enjoy being entertained and donating to a good cause at the same time – they were both giving and getting, which seemed to work well. 'Fuck, that's just what I have been thinking,' he said. 'I could get loads of my mates together and do a big gig to raise some money.' I didn't know it then, but what Bob would go on to do would bring the famine in Ethiopia to the attention of the world.

Back in contact with Bob, and feeling better about myself as I seemed to be making headway with the band and we were now doing the occasional charity event, I didn't say no when he called and invited me to meet him in York.

I'd just got my TVR Taimar and wanted to show it off. It was February 1984, around Valentine's Day, and when I picked him up I gave him a whisky and dry. When he saw the car, his reaction was: 'What the feck is this?'

I laughed, saying, 'It's my new car, you pig!'

'Claire, it's awful!' he said, as he smiled at me with that gorgeous mouth and begrudgingly got in the car.

We set off to a club to which the Rats had been invited for drinks, and that suited me, as I had no intention of going to the hotel with him. I had hoped, now we were speaking on the phone a bit more, that maybe we could just be mates, and that way I could keep him in my life and not have to hang back on the sidelines.

At the club, we were waved straight in, as Bob knew the manager. I remember trying to pay for our drinks with £1 coins; they had just come out and I hated them. We had a great night in the club, just talking and drinking, and, as the band were on the wane by this time, we were pretty much left alone in there. I drank more than I should have and Bob knew I couldn't drive, so I found myself on familiar ground again when he invited me back to the hotel. I said I'd go 'just for a drink' and we left.

By the time we got to the Chase Hotel, the drinks had really kicked in and I decided to climb on to the big saddle that stood outside. Everyone used to attempt this but never could. Laughing, I was soon up in the saddle, giggling. Geldof, however, didn't seem to think it was that funny. 'People are looking, Claire. Get down,' he said.

I dismounted, realising that the age difference between

us was suddenly noticeable, and I didn't like being told what to do by any man.

Entering the hotel, we walked towards the bar. 'We've got to go up to the room now,' Bob said.

I turned to him and replied, 'Who said I was going to your room anyway? And why do we need to go right now?'

He looked a bit embarrassed and said the boys now had to share rooms and he was sharing with Simon Crowe, so, if we wanted to be alone, 'to talk', then we'd need to go up now. I realised times must have got hard for them, because he didn't even have his own room. Feeling a bit pressured and unable to say no, I reluctantly went up to the room, but, after we'd talked and kissed a little, I said I *was* tired and wanted to go to sleep.

And I was tired too of being whatever it was that I meant to him. I knew now that this was it. I'd said it before but now something just clicked in my mind. I deserved more than this and I wouldn't put up with it any longer. We didn't have sex that night – the only time we spent a night together and didn't. It just didn't feel right. Bob fell asleep, and Simon came in and got into his bed. This made me feel really cheap, knowing someone else was in the room, even though we weren't doing anything. It was definitely not how I'd wanted things to be.

Eventually, I drifted off and when I woke up in the morning both of them were still asleep. I looked at Geldof and realised that this was the last time I would see him like this – it was over. I wished I could have taken a picture of him lying there sleeping, or had any pictures of us together, but we'd never got around to it. He looked so beautiful. But I slipped out of the bed gently, not wanting to wake him, and dressed. When I was ready, I tiptoed to the mirror, where I wrote in lipstick: 'It was great, take care, love always, Claire.'

As I let myself out of the room, I knew I'd said my final goodbye. I just couldn't handle being the other woman any more and, as much as I'd kidded myself in the beginning that we'd end up together, that's all I'd become. I felt a really strange mix of emotions as I left the hotel. It really was the end of an era. The last few years, on and off with Geldof, had been great, but now I wanted someone for me and I wanted to make something of myself. I realised I was in love with him and he would never be mine, so I had to let go.

The age-old adage comes to mind: 'If you love someone set them free, and if they love you they'll come back to you.'

I felt wounded that he'd not chosen me as his number one, but I also felt free. Now I could concentrate fully on making *my* life a success and not waste time waiting around for someone who might never come back for me. I'd grown up and the spell was broken.

For about a year, I kept track of Geldof through the press. Band Aid was at Christmas 1984, then 1985 brought Live Aid, which I went to. It was amazing to see something we'd spoken about one night on the phone come to such amazing fruition. I was right at the front as he belted out 'Mondays' to tens of thousands of people in

Hyde Park and millions more all around the world. I cried and cried as the words rang out, and so did others. We were crying for the children of Ethiopia, but a small part of me was crying for my lost love, singing to the world in front of me. I felt proud, but I couldn't *be* proud, because no one knew what we'd shared. It was one of the most spectacular days of my life and I wouldn't have missed it for anything.

Live Aid made me even more determined to go out and find my place in the world. Many of the people who played that day I'd known or still knew (I'd even supported some of them with my bands) and I thought, I want to be up there making a difference – not down here just watching. I wanted to be successful but realised that, as my musical ability was probably limited, I needed to change direction completely.

As I walked out of that stadium, I told myself, Right, I'll show you. I'll show you all.

I was going to make it on my own. I just wasn't sure yet how, or even at what.

# 8

# Change of Plan

Shortly after the beginning of 1985, Great-Grandma Wilson died, followed by my great-uncle Michael, who left me £10,000 in his will – a huge amount of money to a 22-year-old. Since the end of my relationships and the break-up of the band, I'd thrown myself back into the family business, but I was itching to get away from Harrogate and lead a new life. This windfall, I realised, could give me the opportunity to do just that.

I loved spending time with Dad, but I couldn't keep working for him forever; my heart just wasn't in yeast processing! I'd been worrying about how and when to tell him I wanted to leave, as I didn't want him to let him down. As it turned out, he'd sensed how I was feeling and one day, out of the blue, announced that my brother was coming in to take over, with a view to running the whole business when Dad retired. By now, Dad's health wasn't good and he was using a walking stick a lot of the time. So, now I could go and do whatever it was I wanted, Dad told me. He knew better than to ask me what that actually was. Anyway, I still didn't know! Bless him, he'd seen I was desperate for a change, and Piers taking over the business gave me a perfect chance to leave. I had the freedom and the financial security to flee; now all I needed was the opportunity.

They say good things come in threes, and the next day my old friend Sarah Baron, who'd moved to London to work for a model agency some years before, called me for a catch-up. When I told her that with Piers coming into the business I was now free, she suggested that I come down and share her new flat with her. Naturally, I leaped at the chance. London was where everything was happening and the idea of living practically in Soho – Charlotte Street, to be precise – was just too good to resist. With my other close friend Fiona now engaged and living in Greece, it felt like the perfect opportunity to move on, so I said yes instantly. Now I just had to tell my parents.

I called round the next day and broke the news. Mum was a bit upset but neither of them seemed that surprised and said that as long as I was careful they couldn't see any problem. My having lived away from home for the past few years probably made it easier for them to see me go. Dad made me promise I wouldn't blow the money I'd inherited and said that if I had a chance I should buy a flat in London. I said I'd be sensible and went straight home to pack.

As I drove along the country lanes, I wasn't sure exactly

what I was going to do in London but knew I'd have fun finding out. Later that night, I filled my car with the necessities – mainly clothes! – and set off for the bright lights of the booming city that was 1980s London. Thatcher said we could have it all and I was going to get my share.

Moving into Sarah's flat was an amazing change of lifestyle for me. Although it had only one bedroom and was a bit pokey, it was right in the middle of everything and at only £60 a week it left plenty to money for going out – every night. Who wants to stay in when you live right in the West End? Despite being in the thick of it, I immediately felt completely safe, because it was always busy, real 24-hour living. It was great meeting new people every day and night and I was really enjoying the independence that a big city can give you. Soon, we were friendly with our neighbours, and the newsagents opposite got used to us nipping over in our pyjamas. Ours was a very friendly street, where everyone took the time to say hello – not at all like life is now.

Being young and single and regular party animals from our Leeds days, we didn't take long to hit the London nightlife – big time. Our favourite club was the Embassy in New Bond Street, and we practically lived there. We went there most nights and there was always a good crowd in. I was friendly with a greasy rocker who was always on the fruit machine in the corner; he was Lemmy from the band Motorhead. We became really good mates and rumour had it that I was the only woman in London he hadn't tried to sleep with! Not that he would have got anywhere if he had. We just got on because, despite my leather miniskirts and ripped tights, I was still very much one of the boys. My adventures in Amsterdam had taught me how to hang out platonically with the lads.

At that time, the Embassy was really something. Even the waiters were budding pop stars: Mark Shaw, who would go on to have huge hits with Then Jericho, worked at the club. And every night, mixing in with the crowd, were the great and good of London's music scene: Boy George, George Michael, Sigue Sigue Sputnik and Steve Strange were all regulars. Jimmy Pursey of Sham 69 and the Heaven 17 boys were always good for a laugh, and I became good friends with Heaven 17's Glen Gregory and Martin Ware, who invited us to hang out with them at their pads in Notting Hill; they all seemed to live near each other. We'd often go over and marvel at the massive televisions and stereos chart success had brought them.

Glen later introduced me to a mate of his called Spizz, from the band Spizz Energy, who'd just had a massive hit with their single 'Where's Captain Kirk?'. I'd actually met him once before, upstairs at Heaven in Charing Cross Road. At first, I hadn't been too impressed by what looked like the beginnings of a beer belly and his half-spiked hair, but he turned out to be so funny that I ended up finding him attractive. Nothing came of that, though, and this was the first time I'd seen him since then. Spizz wasn't an obvious choice of boyfriend, but he was down-to-earth and we just seemed to get on really well and soon started going out together around Notting Hill, where a lot of good things were happening at the time.

I'd been living in Sarah's flat for a few months when she came home one day and said she had good news and bad news. 'Bad first,' I said. She told me the landlord had sold our building and we were to be evicted in two weeks. 'Jeeze,' I said. 'And the good news?'

'Well, it's good for me, but –' Things were going too well, I thought, as she went on '– I've been offered a job in a model agency in New York, so I won't be needing a flat in London.'

I couldn't believe it. I was happy for her, of course, as it was an amazing opportunity, but all of a sudden things were changing so quickly. Soon I'd have no flat, and Sarah, who'd been my rock, would be halfway across the world – and just when I'd started to feel comfortable. Damn!

Later that day, I told Spizz, who'd taken me for a drink at the Embassy, what had happened. 'Well, why don't you move in with me?' he said. I was quite surprised at the offer because, even though we'd now been together nearly five months, there had been no suggestion that we should live together or that things were that serious. Maybe he sensed I was concerned, because he then tried to play it down. 'Look, I'm moving into a new flat in Notting Hill anyway, so why don't you just come in with me and my mate Justin, who's moving in too? We'll have a right laugh.'

Spizz's idea made sense – we got on well and were

always having a laugh about something. It didn't seem like a big deal to me, as I knew I'd soon be buying my own flat, so moving in with Spizz wouldn't be a long-term commitment. So, although we weren't in love – well, I wasn't – I thought, Why the heck not? 'OK,' I told him. 'Let's do it.'

Within weeks, Sarah had gone off to New York and I was living with my mad pop-star boyfriend in Aldridge Road Villas. Life was far from dull, and we were always up to something. Because the Heaven 17 lot, who lived near by, were from Sheffield, sometimes we'd drive up there and go clubbing. One time, we'd booked into a fancy hotel and had brought with us some magic mushrooms that we'd picked earlier. Soon after eating them, we were all off our faces and got lost in the hotel, accidentally gatecrashing a wedding. The poor guests didn't know what to make of our gurning faces, hysterical laughter and punked-up clothes and hair, but they recognised Glen, so they weren't too upset as we posed for pictures with them.

A lot of people were experimenting with drugs at the time, but I wasn't really interested in trying anything heavy, and luckily no one I hung about with was either. Cocaine and ecstasy were around, but we were more into drinking – a lot!

We had great fun in the Notting Hill flat, but I was becoming very aware that I'd come to London with the goal of making a success of myself one way or another and so far all I'd done was party. My parents wouldn't have been very proud of that, but at least I hadn't squandered the inheritance money and I still had my Harrogate house. In fact, I'd just put it on the market, because Dad had told me it was a good time to sell. The house went really quickly for £19,500 (the following year the one next to it sold for £55,000 – aaarrgh!) and I decided I'd use the money to buy my own place in London.

I'd had a great time living with Spizz but it wasn't a hugely serious relationship for either of us and I felt the time was right to move on, so we stopped seeing each other. When Sarah had left, I'd needed the security of being with someone, and I was grateful to Spizz for that, but I was feeling quite independent now and wanted to go my own way.

After viewing a few flats, I bought one in Camden Road for £42,000. I had wanted one in Notting Hill but there was nothing for less than 60 or 70K, which I couldn't afford. Luckily, I quite liked Camden; it was cool in a less pretentious way. The flat, which was at the Holloway Road end, was quite nice but it was in a right mess – all flock-wallpapered, like an Indian takeaway! The neighbours were young and friendly and I think that helped swing it for me.

Once I'd settled in, I decided it might be nice to have a lodger, and Lol Hammond, who played in a local band called Kiss That, was looking for a place, so he moved in. That helped with the bills and so on, because, although I was always responsible, I could be a little vague. Lol was good mates with Martin Ware's wife, who was also a good friend of mine, so we spent a lot of time over at their house, which was very flash and round the corner from Aldridge Road Villas. Everyone loved that house and there was always someone interesting there.

We were there one day when Martin rang from the studio to say Terence Trent D'Arby, whom he was producing at the time, wanted to use the place to meet some woman he was seeing, and as he was on his way we had to get out quickly. We didn't mind, as he was always really good, letting us chill there, but, wanting to see who Terence's mystery woman was, we decided to hang on a bit longer until he arrived.

Ten minutes later, the door opened and Terence walked in with none other than Paula Yates. We were all surprised, and they seemed quite taken aback that we were still there, so we legged it, laughing. I didn't say anything to the others about how I'd known her, but I certainly felt better knowing she wasn't completely innocent either. It helped me feel less guilty about seeing Geldof for all those years. I suppose what's sauce for the goose...

# 9

# She's Quite Good at That, Isn't She?

Not long after I moved into my flat, I started dating Geoff Bird, at that time better known as Cobalt Stargazer, the lead guitarist of Zodiac Mindwarp. Lemmy had introduced us some months earlier at the Limelight in Charing Cross Road. By now, I'd moved out of my punk phase and had revamped my look as 'sexy rock-chick chic', topping it off by riding a motorbike. And in those days I always had Bon Jovi and Guns N' Roses on my stereo.

Geoff moved in with me almost immediately after we met. We just clicked. It felt quite cool to have a rock-star boyfriend (of my own!), but the down side was that he was always on tour and I hardly saw him offstage during the first year we were together. The plus side was getting to go to all the gigs. When he announced that Zodiac Mindwarp were going to be supporting Guns N' Roses and then Alice Cooper, I knew I'd miss him yet again, but I'd get to take my mates to all the private parties. Spending my nights swanning around with Guns N' Roses guitarist Slash and Jon Bon Jovi was certainly as far from dull as a girl from Harrogate Ladies' College could imagine.

At one of the parties, Jon – I'd always fancied him – really seemed to be trying to make extra-special eye contact with me across the dance floor. I smiled back and was about to go over when Geoff suddenly pulled me over to the other end of the room. Damn! Jon was gorgeous; he was quite small, but in his thin leather trousers he appeared perfectly formed! I was more than a bit disappointed that Geoff had dragged me away.

Then, while Geoff was talking to someone and I was just about to get a drink, Slash came over and accidentally caused another ruckus by flirting with me outrageously – right in front of my boyfriend! Geoff was no wimp, and to his credit he stormed over and told Slash in no uncertain terms that I was 'taken' and he didn't appreciate him trying it on with 'my woman'.

The next thing I knew, they were at each other's throats and had to be dragged apart by minders. I screamed at them to stop and pretended to be horrified that they were fighting over me, but secretly I was loving it. I wouldn't have cheated on Geoff, but knowing you've caught the eye of two of the rock gods you worship certainly works wonders for a girl's ego.

Zodiac Mindwarp's single 'Prime Mover' was doing well in the charts, so the record company decided they needed to shoot a video to go with it. Geoff took me to a couple of the production meetings and I found it really exciting. As I wasn't working, I was happy to have somewhere to go, and even offered to make the tea. Ade Edmondson, from TV's *The Young Ones* and *The Comic Strip*, had been brought in to direct the video and was always nice to everyone. After a few discussions (well, arguments!), the band settled on an idea based on a convent school full of 'good girls gone bad'.

One afternoon, I was passing the drinks round when Ade asked me if I'd like to play one of the 'naughty girls'. I was flattered to be asked and said yes without hesitation. I hadn't done anything like this before but how hard could it be? I wondered. My nameless character was to start off all sweetness and light. Then the band would turn up in a space ship (don't ask me who suggested that) and burst into the school in a tank. Their arrival would spark some sexual reaction, turning us from convent girls into 'sex bitch machines' and we'd suddenly appear with tons of make-up, huge hair and stilettos.

I couldn't wait to start filming. I got my friend Lindsay, girlfriend of Heaven 17's Glen Gregory, involved and we ended up having a blast, as we shot the scenes all slightly drunk after being out late the night before. I was surprised at how comfortable I immediately felt in the film environment. I didn't have any problems taking direction and got all my close-ups in one go, which seemed to impress the crew.

At the end of the shoot, which took a full freezing-cold day, Ade told me he was doing an American video for Elvis

Costello's new single, 'You Ain't Nothing in This Town'. I'd be perfect for this, he said, because, 'Apart from looking right, you've got something that works on camera', and he also knew I could ride a motorbike, which was what was needed for this particular character. Deeply flattered, I accepted his offer at once and went off to tell Geoff. He was really pleased and said I should seriously consider acting as a career. I laughed, saying I'd see how Elvis's video went before I got too excited.

Funnily enough, it wasn't the first time someone had suggested I should try acting. When I was 14, my parents and I were out walking in Harrogate when we saw a film crew at work outside the Royal Baths. I was excited – I'd never seen a real film set before – so we walked over and stood watching for a while.

Always one for a chat, Mum soon got talking to one of the make-up ladies, who told us the film was called *Agatha* – it was about Agatha Christie's real-life disappearance in 1926 – and starred Dustin Hoffman. We all knew who he was and I was just about to ask a million questions when Dustin – we'd seen him in the background filming a running scene but not recognised him – suddenly walked over to the make-up lady we were talking to and asked her for a towel. My dad saw this as an ideal opportunity to introduce the family and immediately offered the actor his hand.

'I bet you're knackered after all that running!' Dad said.

'You bet I am, sir. So, who've we got here then?' Dustin said, as he smiled at Mum and me. Dad introduced us and then Dustin looked at me curiously. 'Gee, she looks like an angel,' he said. 'What do you want to be when you grow up, honey?'

'An actress,' I told him, quite surprising myself, as I normally said 'vet', and causing Dad to laugh and Dustin to smile.

'You've certainly got the face for it, kiddo,' Dustin said, leaning towards me. 'How old are you?

'Fourteen,' Mum told him.

'Well, Claire, come back and see me in six years and I'll see what I can do. You definitely look like an actress to me,' he said, and with that he winked and walked off, leaving us all with dropped jaws. After telling the tale at school the next day, I'd promptly forgotten all about acting until the Zodiac Mindwarp video but now it didn't seem like a bad idea at all – and I hoped that Dustin was right!

A few weeks later, I was at the studio in Wandsworth, south London, to shoot the Elvis Costello video when Ade came over and explained that for my part I had to drive a motorbike and sidecar through 'the gates of hell'.

'OK,' I said, thinking that sounded manageable.

'The thing is, Claire,' he added, 'the gates will be on fire, so you'll have to get it spot on.' He patted my shoulder, then walked off as I kept a forced smile on my face and prayed I wouldn't get it wrong and kill anyone.

The gates in question were made of three large pieces of wood that had been doused with petrol and were now burning away brightly. I looked at the space in the middle and quickly realised that there was literally an inch either side of the flames for me to manoeuvre the bike, with Elvis in the sidecar, safely through. I was a little concerned, to say the least, but poor old Declan – Elvis's real name – was terrified and kept repeating, 'My God, you can drive, Claire, can't you? Please tell me you can drive!' I just laughed and told him not to worry.

Once I'd got over the surprise, I knew I could do it, as I was quite handy on my own bike. Besides, if I showed Elvis I was nervous, he might just climb out of the sidecar, saying he didn't trust me, and that would be me out of a job. So I had to get it right.

The finishing touches were being put to my hair and make-up – sexy big hair and bright lips – when Harry Enfield, who had just had a big hit with his comic character Loadsamoney, came over to say hello. He was playing a game-show host to my character Vanna White in a later scene and he took the time to speak to me before we started, which I thought was really nice. I couldn't believe it. Here I was, not an actress – that I was aware of – playing opposite one of the country's top TV comedians and about to drive Elvis Costello through the flaming gates of hell!

At least life's never dull, I thought, as I walked over to meet the guy who owned the bike I'd be using. I was just starting to feel quite confident about the fire scene when I suddenly noticed he had lost an arm, which meant that all the controls would be on one side instead of both. Shit! I thought. I bloody hope he didn't lose it on this stunt! It was going to be hard enough as it was, but now I knew about the bike's controls I was really worried. But I didn't let Elvis know.

We got on the bike as a new set of gates were set on fire. Right, no going back now, I told myself as the director called 'action' and I sped off as skilfully as I could, screeching towards what looked like death. Luckily, disaster was averted! I passed through perfectly and we got the scene in the first take. Everyone applauded and Elvis looked like he could breathe again.

After the shoot wrapped later that night, I left the studio even more sure of my interest in this acting lark. On set, everyone had raved about my professionalism, so maybe this was something I could make a living at. On the way home, I remembered that Dad had done a bit of acting when he was younger. He appeared in the first performance of John Osborne's *Look Back in Anger* at the Bradford Civic before I was born, so, while it didn't exactly run in the family, it was something that my own flesh and blood had at least dipped a toe into.

The next day, Geoff, who'd been really lovely about me getting the second video, set off on tour again with Zodiac Mindwarp. I really missed him but, on the plus side, being on my own for a while pushed me to see if I could follow up on the taste of acting I'd just had. Ade had said that I should sign up for an acting course, as it would help me get work in the future. He clearly knew what he was talking about, as he was never off the telly, so after weighing up a few courses in *The Stage* – I'd been told this was the actor's bible – I decided on the Actors' Institute in Islington, which was the closest to my flat.

Debbie Harry, who had always been one of my biggest inspirations, had recently started acting and I'd loved Madonna in *Desperately Seeking Susan*, and I definitely wanted to give it a go. When I walked into the induction class, I was in for a big surprise – no Debbie Harrys or Madonnas here! I'd half-expected to see a lovely room with plush sofas and piles of scripts, full of Patsy Kensit wannabes (*Absolute Beginners* had just come out) and chiselled men who looked like Nick Kamen talking about 'the arts'. But what I found was actually a grotty old school room with wallpaper that had seen better days and uncomfortable old chairs behind matching desks. It wasn't a cheap course either. They could at least have given us cushions, I thought, as my bum went numb on the wooden seat.

The people were as much of a shock as the decor – a real hotchpotch from all walks of life, all ages, all sizes. I'm not too sure about this, I thought, as I looked around, but I reminded myself not to go on first impressions and resolved to throw myself into the classes. While the course certainly wasn't one of the most prestigious, the Actors' Institute did specialise in 'Acting on Camera', which even the poshest drama school, RADA, wasn't doing at that time, so I stuck with it.

Every class I attended felt very strange to me. One week, we'd be improvising that we'd landed on the moon and there was suddenly no oxygen, so you'd 'die'. Another time we'd go to the zoo and then come back and mimic the animals. You'd have people being baboons rubbing their bottoms along the floor, which was not a pretty sight. I chose to be a giraffe, as it meant I didn't have to crouch down on the floor.

I enjoyed the on-camera scenes the best. Well, not all of them. I remember one particularly horrible bed scene I had to do with a man who was as hairy as one of the gorillas we'd seen at the zoo. I had to cuddle up to him in bed and he smelled as bad as any gorilla could, so I was nearly sick each time we went for a take.

Week after week, we continued doing these acting exercises and, although after six months I felt I had learned some skills, I was starting to feel I'd had enough. One day, we were told we were all to be chocolates. One by one, the teacher went round all the group and asked them what they were. Big Beryl, a dinner lady from King's Cross, was standing stiff as a board. 'I'm an After Eight mint,' she trilled. The teacher smiled as I cringed. Next was Derrick, who was cuddling himself. 'And what is Derrick?' said the teacher. 'A Walnut Whip!' replied Derrick. There must be more to acting than this, I was thinking.

When the teacher reached me, I knew I'd had enough. I was standing normally and not pulling any shape that I was aware of. She looked at me and asked enthusiastically, 'What sort of chocolate are you, Claire?'

I looked around the room at what looked like a workout with Mad Lizzy from breakfast television and then back at her. 'A stale one,' I said, and walked out.

I knew I should have finished the course and I knew it

was really well intentioned but I felt I was getting nowhere fast. I'd already done two professional jobs before I joined and I now had on tape quite a good collection of on-screen clips from the class. To my mind, that was enough to be going on with and I just couldn't stand being a chocolate or a monkey any more. I wanted to be like Margaret Rutherford. I'd loved her in *The Wicked Lady* and I couldn't see her bouncing around calling herself a Creme Egg.

One week, I spotted an advert in *The Stage* for a company called Traffic of the Stage, who were casting for a new production. *The Pleasure Principle* seemed a quite interesting play and the casting breakdown said they wanted an attractive actress with a sexy edge – well, that sounded like me – so I phoned and was asked to audition the next day. Since I'd never been to a theatre audition, I wasn't sure what to expect and I just decided I'd give it my best shot and see what happened.

The sexy bit in the ad was easy, though. I picked out a black Lycra top and a matching mini with a red stripe down the side (very in at the time!). The next day, when I walked into the casting room, I realised it had never entered my head that there would be hundreds of women desperate to be in this low-budget production. I was quite sure I wouldn't get it once I'd seen the other girls, who all looked rather smart holding their CVs. OK, Claire, I told myself. Just enjoy it.

I read the script they gave me and, because I'm lucky enough to have a good memory, I found I could read it once and then go with it, which gave me the chance to

*bove*: Me, the exploding baby, at six months old!

*elow left*: Never a girly girl, here I am getting my hands dirty in the garden with Dad.

*elow right*: With my brother Piers on holiday in Jersey – we could swim without
·mbands even at this young age.

My father, Captain John Seed, by the fireplace with our gorgeous Labrador Kim.

*bove*: A book at bedtime with Mum and Piers.

*elow*: The Manor House, Tong, my maternal grandparents' *me* – very *Wuthering Heights*! *Inset*: With my maternal *andmother*, Ella, in the garden at The Manor House.

*Above*: The coolest set of wheels in Yorkshire!

*Below left*: Daddy's girl, relaxing on holiday.

*Below right*: Off to a fancy dress party with Piers. I'm wearing my Godfather's rally-driving gear.

A family with a passion for all things equestrian …

*Above*: Mum outside Roseberry Cottage…

*Below*: …and showing Piers and me how it's done.

*Above*: Riding my beloved Rocket at Ripley Show.

*Below*: Eventing on my dad's horse, Horace, aged 14.

GOOD DRAWING WEATHER. Girls of West End School, Harrogate, take advantage of the sunshine yesterday to have an outdoor art lesson drawing daffodils on the West Park Stray, Harrogate. Left to right are Claire Seed, eight, Victoria Farnell, seven and Caroline Bostock, eight. (A Yorkshire Post picture.)

*bove*: My first brush with fame.

*elow*: My house photo from Harrogate Ladies' College. I was in Balliol House and that's e in the second row, second from the right. My good friend Fiona is in the third row, xth from the right.

*Above*: Piers and I in our early punk days.

*Below*: Me and my disastrous haircut – I'm the English Rose to Piers' dark and mysterious.

look each of the company members I was playing to in the eye as I delivered the lines. It seemed to go OK and after I'd finished they thanked me and asked if I would mind wearing just a bra in one scene of the show, as this was something that the character did. I laughed, saying I didn't mind at all. They said they'd call me, so off I went, not expecting to hear anything from them but glad not to have embarrassed myself too badly.

Later that night, to my complete surprise, John Cooper, who owned the company, called and said if I wanted the part it was mine; and, if so, could I start rehearsals in two weeks? My first audition and I'd got the job! I hadn't known at the time, but John had been the only one of the three company members who had wanted me in the show, although I couldn't have blamed them, as my CV was practically bare. He was convinced I had 'something' and had really fought my corner.

My excitement over my first theatre job was marred a little by the rude awakening I received when I turned up to work and realised I hadn't read the advert properly. One of the conditions of doing the play in the evening was that during the day the company of actors all had to tour schools and perform TIE (Theatre in Education). I was not prepared for that, and it was a hard slog. We had to make all our own costumes and then run drama workshops with the children – I felt I should be attending one, not teaching one – but I did my best and no one seemed to complain.

God, how quickly life can change. It didn't seem so long ago that I was crammed into a van with six boys, stoned on weed, touring Amsterdam as a punk singer, and now I was teaching schoolchildren the importance of drama. Most of the kids were sweet, and the teenage boys, who had previously never had any interest in drama, suddenly seemed rather taken with the subject when I walked in dressed in cave-girl rags and announced I was Stig of the Dump. It ended up being quite fun and was a steep learning curve, but very hard work. We were working from 9am to 4pm in the schools, then travelling back to London and performing the show from 7.30 until 10.15pm – and not earning a penny. But I didn't mind, as I knew it wasn't for long and I was adding valuable points to my CV.

The evening show was at the New End Theatre in Hampstead. It was a real culture shock to be in front of London theatregoers after surfing the moshpits at punk gigs, but I loved it and seemed to get quite a good reaction from the audience. And, mid-run, someone brought in a copy of *The Stage* to show me that I was on the front cover – in my bra! I ran around the dressing room screaming, 'Oh my God!' It was so exciting. A lot of people bought the newspaper at that time and many I hadn't seen in ages called me up to tell me how cool it was. My friend Helen, from my drama class, and Clarissa, who ran my favourite restaurant in Camden, Ruby in the Dust, rang to say, 'Nice bra!'

My first job and I'd got a front cover! Yes! That cover also brought me my first fan mail. Over the next two weeks, I received a dozen or so letters from senders ranging from a lovely college boy, proposing undying love, to a scary Arab who said that 'the aliens had taken his wife to Mercury' and asking why I was wearing her bra!

Geoff was still on tour and I knew by now that they all 'played away' while away from home, so when I found myself attracted to and then having a brief fling with Marcus Gilbert, the lead man in the play, I didn't feel like I was being too unfaithful. It was just a bit of fun. I'd stay at his house in Earl's Court and we'd talk about acting, which was fascinating to me and was what drew me to him. The knowledge and talent he seemed to have made him sexy in my eyes.

Our fling only lasted the length of the run and then Marcus moved to America and acted in a few movies, before coming back to appear in ITV's adaptation of Jilly Cooper's novel *Riders*. I wasn't bothered when it ended, as I still loved Geoff and just wanted him to come home to me.

Before *The Pleasure Principle* ended, I was told that career-wise the best thing to do next was to write to lots of agents and get as many people in to see the play as I could. I sent out about a hundred letters, along with an old head shot that was quite punky. My current hairstyle was less wild – I'd gone back to my natural blonde.

Before long, an agent called Heidi Cook invited me to visit her. She was holding auditions at the Donmar Warehouse in Covent Garden, she told me, and if I wanted to be considered for her agency I should come along, having prepared a classic and a modern piece. I asked Helen for advice here, as I wasn't too up on which material might be appropriate, and she helped me work on the two pieces the night before. I knew an agent was what I needed, so I went along to the Donmar and did my very best, performing Kate from *The Taming of the Shrew*, which was probably a bit ambitious, as well as having a stab at Marilyn Monroe in *Bus Stop*. Once I'd finished and answered a few questions and filled in some forms, I was waved off with no clue as to whether I'd been accepted or not.

Afterwards, I was excited and nervous. I hoped I hadn't come across as too desperate. When would I find out? Would it be tomorrow? Or in a week's time? But I knew I'd done my best, so I just thought, *Che sera sera*. What will be will be. I wanted the chance to attend more castings and even get a dream job, and I knew I had little chance without an agent, but, when Geoff came home a few days later, we were so busy catching up that I just put it to the back of my mind.

A few weeks later, a letter arrived saying that I'd been accepted. I now had my own agent. Before long, I was appearing on lots of the TV shows that I'd previously watched.

But it wasn't all good news. When my Grandpa Charlie died, I had to go home and accompany the family to Torquay for his funeral; it was a really sad occasion. Grandma Kathleen moved up to Yorkshire to be near the family, so at least she wouldn't be on her own.

Back in London, I was booked to appear in *Alas Smith and Jones*, as the token sexy girl. By now, I could do a nice line in 'the tart with a heart' and in one episode I played Mel's frustrated girlfriend, who's waiting for him in bed feeling randy. He's more interested in fixing his motorbike, covered in oil, in the bedroom, so to tempt him over I pull back the sheets to reveal my lingerie. It seems to work but he grabs a kebab from the side table before kissing me – and I get a mouth full of spillage. We had to do that scene three or four times and I was beginning to feel sick after tasting that kebab over and over. But Mel was really nice to me and I was having a great time learning how everything works on a TV set. I wasn't one of those who'd just turn up, do the scene and then leave.

I used to hang around and watch where the cameras were and how the director and crew worked. Soon I learned that, if you made an effort with the crew, they would help you out if you needed it. Sometimes, directors don't explain things as clearly as they might and a helpful crew member will always keep an eye out for you if you've taken the time to be polite and respectful to them. I also saw that it doesn't hurt to stay in with the lighting crew, as harsh light is definitely not a girl's best friend.

The work continued to roll in and because I could ride both horses and motorbikes I'd been advised to start working on my stunt card, as there weren't many female stunt women in the business and the money was really good. I was halfway through the exams – I'd passed the swimming and horse-riding sections – when I was sent up to try out for *Batman*, starring Michael Keaton and Jack Nicholson. I did a motorbike test ride at Pinewood Studios, as I was auditioning to be part of a group of Hell's Angels who rode around Gotham City terrorising everyone. I got the part and was soon riding round the amazing set all night.

On my third day, I met Jack Nicholson, who was really not my type at all. I switched off when he talked about his recent big-game hunting trip to Africa, so, despite his harmless flirting, I was not on his wavelength.

The money was amazing – every night I was making nearly a previous month's salary. I couldn't believe my luck when, as soon as I finished on that film, I was immediately hired to stunt-ride in two films based on novels by Barbara Cartland. Things were really shaping up, I thought to myself one morning on set. But, of course, that's just when something bad always happens to spoil it.

Geoff had just come back from another tour, this time with Belinda Carlisle. He'd been a bit distant since coming home and had been going out a lot without me. We'd been invited to stay for Christmas by my parents and, as we set off, he seemed to pull himself together. They hadn't met Geoff yet and it was important to me that they liked him. On the way there, he surprised me by telling me he loved me and giving me a gorgeous tasselled leather jacket. Maybe things were going to be all right between us after all.

My parents took to him straight away, which was a bit of a surprise, as on first meeting him they joked that they wanted to poke him to see if he was real. His goatee, long, straggly hair, tattoos and leather suit were not quite Harrogate chic, but they'd begun to give in to my unusual ways and said, as long as I was happy and whoever I was with treated me well, they were happy for me. Geoff might have looked wild but he was actually from a good family and was able to relate to my parents well, so we had a perfect few days.

On the last night, he proposed to me on bended knee in the garden – this was the first I'd heard of us getting married – but it seemed like a good idea at the time and I did love him, so I accepted.

Was I to be a rock star's wife after all?

Christmas had passed in a lovely blur, but once we were back in London Geoff went straight back to being strangely distant. When I confronted him, he denied that there was anything wrong with the way he was behaving towards me – I felt I had no choice but to call off our engagement.

Geoff didn't argue. He went back on tour with Belinda, which I was less than pleased about, and, although we didn't officially split up, our relationship was now far from healthy. But, still in love with him, I buried my head in the sand and threw myself back into my work.

It was now 1989 and I was busier than ever, doing guest spots on TV shows and adverts. Everything was going well career-wise and, although I hadn't had any lead roles since the play, I was confident that the right thing would come along soon. In September, it appeared that it had.

One Tuesday morning, I got a strange call from my agent Heidi, who, instead of the customary pleasantries, just said in a serious tone, 'Claire, I want to ask you something and I need you to be completely honest with me.'

I gripped the phone and sat down in a panic. 'OK,' I managed, wondering what the hell she was going to say.

'On your CV you've listed that you can ride,' she said. 'Now listen, honey, everyone always ticks every box for fear of losing out on a job, but I need to know, can you really ride a horse and, if so, how well?'

I laughed and relaxed – I wasn't in trouble after all. 'Heidi, trust me,' I replied. 'You don't have to worry about that – I can definitely ride a horse!'

She sounded relieved, as if she'd called lots of girls before me who'd lied about what they could do. Luckily, I wasn't one of them – well, not about being able to ride anyway!

'Great. Well, get yourself up to Yorkshire tomorrow – you've got an audition for a new regular character in *Emmerdale*,' she explained.

'OK,' I said, writing down the details of the casting, which would be at the *Emmerdale* studios in Leeds. Once I'd put down the receiver, I had a strange feeling that I really wanted this job, even though I didn't know what the character was like. The idea of going home suddenly seemed really appealing. I'd had no idea I felt like that until that phone call, when I was suddenly aware that I'd had enough of London. Occasionally, I'd watched *Emmerdale* and knew it was set in the Dales, and I thought, Well, I'm from that type of area and background. Maybe I can do this.

I rang Mum and Dad, who were over the moon and started saying how fantastic it would be if I got the part and moved closer to them. They had shown some interest in others roles I'd done and had come to see me in *The Pleasure Principle*, but I was quite taken aback by their reaction towards this part. They seemed to be taking the idea of me being an actress seriously. It also made me think how happy they'd be to have me closer to them, and I was touched.

Fate appeared to be playing a hand again and everything was hinting that this mysterious part could be the next piece in the jigsaw of my life. But I was already beginning to worry about what it would mean for me and Geoff if I got the part and moved back to Yorkshire. I'd already made up my mind that, even if I didn't get the part, I'd be heading home anyway. Geoff was always away on tour so I decided it was time to put my career first for once. I was 26 and it was time for a change again.

I dropped by Heidi's office and picked up the script and the breakdown. The character I was going for was called Kim and was part of a new family, the Tates, who were to be introduced into the sleepy village of Emmerdale to shake things up a bit. The father and son had already been cast and now they were looking for the two Tate women. Kim was married to a much older man, Frank, and it was hinted that she'd married him for money but that the audience wouldn't be aware of this for some time to come.

So, the Tates were to move in and take over the village – it sounded good to me! As for Kim, she sounded like a strong character who would bring a touch of *Dynasty* to the Dales. It was well known that the show was undergoing a revamp, and with big changes in the offing I was now more determined than ever to win the part of this woman Kim Tate.

# 10

# A Bitch is Born

I stayed with my parents the night before the *Emmerdale* audition and woke up the next morning full of nerves, which was very unlike me.

The audition wasn't until 3.30 that afternoon, so I had plenty of time to prepare. I spent most of the morning working out how I thought Kim might look and dress. It said on the script that, although she was now 'the lady of the manor', she was really a working-class girl made good, so I knew she'd have a style that was far from bland.

Rummaging through old clothes I'd left at home, and some of my mum's too, I eventually found a two-tone riding jacket I thought would look perfect. I put it together with a white shirt, a long black skirt and riding boots. When I looked in the mirror, I was shocked at who I saw – it didn't look like me at all, but hopefully *I* looked like *her*. After giving my outfit approving glances – they'd always wanted me to dress like this – Mum wished me luck and Dad said I could drive his new BMW 325 into Leeds, which was sweet of him. Looking back, it must have really set the right tone when I drove up to the studios.

After finally finding a parking space, I looked around for the studio entrance. By now, I was running late and had just a few minutes to spare. I searched around everywhere but couldn't find the way in. I was beginning to panic that I was going to miss my slot when I finally noticed a little door behind one of the cars. I dashed straight through into a little corridor, ending up slap bang in the middle of a bunch of dinner ladies. I'd burst into the kitchen! Really embarrassed, I explained what I was there for and one kind lady said she'd show me the way. As she led me through a packed canteen filled with the cast and crew, I felt so silly with everyone looking at me, but I thanked her profusely for helping me.

When I reached the correct door, a sniffy-looking receptionist greeted me. 'Oh, hello,' she said in a breathy tone that sounded more than a bit like Fenella Fielding, adding dryly, 'And where have you come from?' The ridiculousness of it all cracked me up, but I managed to explain what I'd done and why I was there. She took my name and motioned me towards a row of chairs where another five or six girls were sitting. Years later, the receptionist, Julie Bywell, and I became mates and her voice, which was a fake telephone one, became the butt of many jokes.

By the look of the other girls, they were also there for

the two Tate women's roles. I was just about to take a seat with them when the studio door opposite us opened and Glenda McKay – I knew she played Rachel in the show – walked through, smiled and said hello as she passed. Oh, that's sweet, I thought. Everyone's going to be really nice. Then the door opened again and Malandra Burrows, who played Kathy, walked through. A few moments later, Frazer Hines came by and started chatting to us about the show and wishing us luck. I knew him vaguely through my parents and he told me to send them his best. It was surreal, to say the least – I'd watched these actors on telly and now I was auditioning to be in a show with them.

I was about to reread the script I had with me, when I glanced across the room and noticed one girl sitting opposite. She was dressed in jeans, boots, waistcoat and cap and her hair was done in a French plait. Oh, God, I thought, she looks just like someone off the show already – I bet it goes to her. Maybe I'd gone too far with my *Dynasty* theme, whereas she really did look the part – or so I thought.

Oh well, I told myself, if I can just learn something from the audition I'll have to be happy with that. My thoughts were interrupted by the receptionist telling me to go through. Once in the room, I was told I would be reading with the actor Norman Bowler, who had been cast as Kim's husband, Frank. When I was introduced to him, I have to admit, I was more than a little disappointed. I'd known that he was going to be an older man but I had hoped for more of a Richard Gere look and Norman, although not hideous, was far from sexy. I knew I'd have to kiss him in the scene – it was in the script – but I thought, I'll close my eyes and deal with that later!

Norman introduced himself to me and was polite but had clearly read with lots of women for this role, as he seemed to be going through the motions. I knew instantly, from the decision to cast him as Frank Tate, that Kim had definitely married him for his money. But Norman had a strong presence, so once we started reading I found it quite easy to relate to him in character. Despite the drama of getting lost on the way in, seeing the stars and the fact that I was sure the girl I'd seen in the corridor would get the part, I'd forgotten all my nerves and was determined to enjoy it.

We finished the scene with the kiss, which I chose to deliver as a peck. I felt it went quite well but Norman didn't offer any inside information and I was asked by the director to wait outside. As I went back into the corridor, I noticed most of the girls, including the one I'd thought looked perfect, leaving. I sat down and was left alone there for at least 20 minutes. There were now no more girls coming or going and I was the only one left. I began to think that maybe I'd misheard the director and he hadn't asked me to wait, so I went to check with the receptionist, who said that if they'd told me to wait that's what I should do.

She was a bit friendlier with me now that it was just the two of us, and told me that the actor Peter Amory, who had already been cast to play Frank's son and heir, Chris Tate, had also been reading all day with a mix of the possible Kims and Zoes (Zoe was the Tate daughter/sister) all day. Apparently, he had read with one girl who, he had told everyone, he really wanted to play the part of Kim. I don't think the receptionist was trying to be rude, but I felt sure they must have simply forgotten to send me home if that was the case. I was just about to leave when Stuart Doughty, the producer, came in and asked me to come back into the room. I followed him through and was asked to sit down.

'You can ride, can't you, Claire?' Stuart asked.

'Yes, no problem,' I answered, nodding my head frantically, and with that they offered me the part, on an eight-month contract. You start on Monday, they said.

Blimey! I couldn't believe this was happening and suddenly I wanted to cry. I was shaking but trying desperately not to show it, as I didn't want them to think I was some wimp and change their minds. Thanking them effusively, I promised I wouldn't let them down.

Somehow, I managed to find my way to the car park. The gravel under my feet seemed to be dancing about as I walked towards the car. Shit! I've actually pulled it off – but will I be able to do it? My mind was racing and I wanted to run and tell my mum and dad. I stumbled towards the car and bumped straight into Glenda. 'Sorry!' I said. She laughed and asked me how it went. 'I think I'll be joining you,' I said quietly, not wanting to tempt fate until I'd seen a contact. Glenda smiled again and said she hoped to see me soon then. This is amazing, I was thinking as I got into the car. And everyone seems really friendly too! I drove straight to the village shop, bought two bottles of champagne and used the payphone outside to call Heidi.

'I've got it,' I said.

'I know, they've just called,' she replied, as if I was telling her I'd got a job in Tesco. She confirmed that I'd be starting the following Monday and that it would probably be best to find somewhere to live close to set, as the contract was for eight months, with the possibility, if the character was popular, of becoming permanent.

As I put down the phone, my mind was all over the place. I was wondering what life on a TV show would be like and what it would do to my already strained relationship with Geoff. I parked at my parents' house and Dad came to the office door to greet me, clearly expecting news. I walked over to him and described the girl I'd seen waiting to audition, telling him how she looked just the type they'd be looking for, hanging my face down as if things hadn't gone my way. (It seems to me this is a British joke thing we all do.)

Dad smiled and said, 'Never mind, you'll find something else' and then I said, 'But she didn't get it, Dad – I did!' He realised what I'd said and started laughing – he actually had tears in his eyes. When Mum came back, we did the same thing to her and she burst into tears. We drank the champagne together, still in a state of disbelief.

Very soon, the realisation of how many changes I would have to make was sinking in. Not least, the next morning I would have to get back to London and tell Geoff.

After a night of bizarre dreams, some of which involved finding out that I hadn't really got the part after all, and one where Annie Sugden attacked me with a pitchfork dressed like Ellie May from *The Beverly Hillbillies*, I drove back to London and went straight to see Heidi. She explained that I was to be on £320 per episode – wow, I was rich! – and that I'd be needed most weekdays and occasional weekends. She asked me if I intended to commute or move closer to set, as they were very keen on punctuality. I told her I wasn't sure yet and that I would get back to her when I'd made up my mind. Once I've seen Geoff, more like, I thought.

In fact, when I told Geoff, he surprised me by being great about it. He hugged me, saying he was really proud and that it was now my turn to work away and that he'd still be there for me – if I wanted him. So, a day or so later, we packed my little MG with as much stuff as it could fit and kissed each other goodbye. He carried my stuff out for me, bless him, and we hugged at the gate. He said he would have come with me for my first few days, but, since they were recording the new album, he just couldn't get out of it.

I waved to him as I drove off, wondering if we'd survive the distance and yet knowing only time would tell. Once again, events had taken a dramatic turn, but I had no idea just how much drama Kim Tate was to inject into my life.

# 11

# War of the Roses

On my first day of rehearsals, I met Leah Bracknell, who'd been cast as my stepdaughter Zoe Tate. I liked Leah instantly; she was funny and friendly and we soon clicked. But, unlike me, she was quite scared of horses, which was doubly unfortunate for her, as the first scene of the two of us to be shown on *Emmerdale* was Kim and Zoe racing across country on horseback, to see who can get to Home Farm first. The Tate boys have already arrived and we are about to join them. We set off in different directions, and Kim tries to get there first, which, considering she is Zoe's stepmother, shows her competitive streak right from the off.

I'd been given a chestnut horse called Tilley, who had seemed lovely all morning, so I wasn't too nervous when they set up for my second scene, which was Kim cantering through a field unaware that coming the opposite way is

Seth Armstrong, on a bicycle. She only sees him at the last minute and narrowly misses him.

Now you can pretty much take full control of a motorbike, but no one, not even the best jockey in the world, is ever in 100 per cent control of a horse. We started the scene and got to the part where I was due to pull away, when Tilley suddenly reared up over Stan Richards (Seth) and looked set to knock him off his bike for real. Luckily, I was able to gain control over her and save the situation at the last moment, but it had been a very close call, for if she'd hit him he would have been seriously hurt. So it seemed they were right to hire a trained horsewoman in this role, as accidents were clearly going to happen.

Funnily enough, this broke the ice and made me forget my nerves. I got on really well with Stan, who would become one of my closest friends on set, and from then on he would always tell the story of how I saved his life. I don't think I did that, but anyway no harm was done. So that was my first day on *Emmerdale*. Kim had arrived.

During the first few weeks of filming, I was so exhausted after each long day that all I did was eat and sleep. I was such a rookie – this was my first real acting job – and I soon found that the demands of soap leave very little time for mistakes, though I still managed to make a few. My first scene filmed (not the transmitted one) was with Frazer Hines in a Land Rover and was rather embarrassing. We'd just been set up to do another take when the assistant director said, 'Right, let's go again', meaning everyone get ready, but I started speaking without waiting for 'Action!'

Everyone laughed, because I'd shown my lack of experience, but you learn quickly when you're embarrassing yourself, and I never made that mistake again. Luckily, Frazer was the perfect gent and had been totally supportive, though I'd soon discover that not all actors are like that.

The hectic schedule left no time for a social life, but I didn't mind, as I was more happy to throw myself into my new 'family'. By now, I'd met Peter Amory, who played my stepson, Chris Tate. As I'd already learned from Julie the receptionist that Peter had wanted another actress to play Kim, I was a bit wary of him and, while we got on OK on set, we didn't really hit it off as well as we might have.

Little did he know that, if he had got his way, that really would have changed our destinies forever.

The Tates were quite a nice family to start with and some of our first episodes, which went out in December, showed us happily together around the Christmas tree, all laughing and joking. In fact, we continued to seem happy enough for quite a while. At first, we didn't make the impact that we eventually would, but the viewers seemed to like us, whereas in the storyline the villagers certainly didn't. Frank Tate quickly became quite ruthless, and gradually the rest of the family followed suit.

It was around this time that I was invited to do my first television interview. I'd been sent over to Manchester to see Eamon Holmes on the daytime chat show he was hosting at the time. He was really lovely and we became friends. When the programme went out that night, a few people commented on it and it brought in a few more requests for interviews, even though I hadn't appeared on screen yet as Kim Tate. No one was really paying much attention at the time, so media interest wasn't too intrusive – just the odd magazine shoot and then back to work.

Having previously felt that Norman hadn't taken to me as much as he might have in the audition or in my first few scenes with him, I now heard from other cast members that he was referring to me as ' the untrained one'. This really annoyed me, as, while I might not have been fully drama-trained, I was doing my best and I didn't seem to be getting any complaints from any of the producers, the other actors or in the increasing fan mail I was receiving.

Although Norman never actually said anything like that to my face, I accepted that he'd been saying it but tried not to let it bother me, thinking, I'm just at the start of my career and he's obviously on the last run, so forget it. The tension often mounted on set, as he could be quite a confident performer in our scenes together and had a habit of standing in front of you while delivering his lines. It was nothing anyone else would generally notice but just enough to try to upstage you. Luckily, I caught on to his antics early and soon learned what to watch out for. After some time of this, I thought, OK, matey boy, if you want it like that, you can have it like that.

I never actually showed him any attitude or let him know that he annoyed me, but whenever we had kissing scenes – and in the early days we had quite a few – I would munch on raw garlic before each shot. He used to grimace after each take but never said anything back. It was childish but it worked. Ha! We were becoming like the couple in *The War of the Roses*. One of the main problems – I thought so, anyway, and so did others – was that, while we were both good in our roles, there was no real chemistry between us.

In the end, this is probably what helped Kim evolve into the character she became. If she'd looked happy being at home playing the dutiful wife, she might not have strayed – which was when she first really came to life.

I was told that originally Kim was to have been married to Chris but the producers decided that she was so ruthless she would have cut out the 'middle man' and gone straight for the father. This was why Chris always had a thing for Kim, while at the same time despising her. Kim felt the same and their love-hate relationship became a firm favourite with the audience. Whenever I was in scenes with Peter, I noticed I was being given harder lines than normal and could see a chance of a change of direction for Kim. When I got those lines, I decided, I would play them even harder than they'd been written, because bad girls were always the best parts and Kim certainly seemed to be – with a little push – heading in that direction.

I'd become quite friendly with Fionnuala Ellwood, who played Lynn Whiteley, the show's current bitch. So, when she decided to leave, about a year after I'd joined (I thought it was a bit early to leave, as *Emmerdale* had not really found its primetime place – we were still on at 6pm and the industry was rumouring the show might be in trouble), suddenly lots more of my scenes seemed to be written 'harder' and before long all of Kim's dialogue became stronger and more bitchy. Kim was patently being groomed as queen bitch of the Dales – and I was loving every minute.

It was no surprise that my press requests were picking up. *Emmerdale*'s publicity department was run by a lovely girl called Shanti Bhatia, who always made sure that Kim got a lot of coverage in the papers and magazines, and I enjoyed working with her more and more as the attention grew. And, boy, did it grow!

# 12

# Lady Rides Again

Even though Kim's storylines were hotting up, I was only working about three days a week, so I had plenty of free time. This worked out really well because my friend Clare Pears, who'd been on my secretarial course, had moved back from the States to work close by, for the trainer Charlie Booth, and she had invited me over to his yard to 'ride work' on Wednesdays and Saturdays. [Ride work is a racing term for days when you 'work' the horses – galloping, twice a week – as opposed to just exercising them – cantering – on the other days, which is known as 'riding out'.]

Clare suggested that, because I had plenty of time off, I should apply for an amateur jockey's licence so that I could race in my spare time. Having never 'race ridden' before, I had no idea how much preparation I'd have to do to get that licence. In the end, many weeks were spent jogging along country roads in the freezing cold in a sweat suit, not to mention the rigorous programme of cycling and swimming. But I'm not a person who does things by halves, so even though it was tough I stuck with it and eventually gained my licence.

Kieren Fallon, an up-and-coming Irish jockey, had just joined Jimmy Fitzgerald's yard and Jimmy was a good friend of Charlie's, so I would often see him on the gallops, where he and the rest of the male jockeys would make fun of me. 'What's an actress doing on a racehorse then?' Kieren shouted one day.

'Riding it,' I said and rode off laughing. I knew they thought I was stuck up – I'd been told – so I didn't bother mincing my words. I was finding my feet in the racing set and soon discovered it was very much a man's world.

For my first outing, I was entered into a charity race at Newmarket with ex-jockeys like John Francome, Walter Swinburn senior, Eddie Hide and Frazer Hines, who also rode as an amateur. I was terrified during the race, but doing my best I managed to finish fourth and I was really pleased, though I knew there was loads of room for improvement. As I dismounted, I didn't fall over with 'shaky legs', as Charlie had said I would, which was a relief, even though I was riding with longer stirrups than John Wayne! I'd even managed to beat John Francome, who cheekily told the handful of local hacks there that 'the one reason I wouldn't go past her was because I liked the view so much'. That gave me a laugh when I saw it in the papers the next day.

One afternoon, Clare called to let me know she was looking after Desert Orchid, one of the most famous horses of all time, and a favourite of mine. 'Dessie', owned by Richard Burridge, had been brought up to Fryup, on the North Yorkshire Moors, from David Elsworth's yard in Whitsbury, Hampshire. He would be staying there until he went back into training and Clare would do the road work before he returned south. I started to go to the stables on Sundays, where Clare and I would each ride one of the other horses while Richard rode Dessie. Henrietta, his girlfriend, and now his wife, would cook, and Mary Reveley and David Elsworth would come over for lunch. A perfect way to spend a Sunday.

Richard rang me one morning to ask if I'd like to come for lunch... and ride Dessie. 'Would I ever!' I practically threw on my jodhpurs and drove straight over to his yard. Clare met me at the gate and asked if I could groom Dessie before I took him out. Damn! I thought, knowing there had to be a catch. Well, as beautiful a horse as he was, he was well known for being difficult to groom, and in fact Clare had often mentioned that you had to tie him up tightly as he loved to bite human flesh! But, after one failed attempt to nip me, Dessie seemed quite happy to let me 'dress him over' and once we were tacked up Richard set off on him while I followed on Irish Orchid. After a couple of miles, Richard suggested we swap. I can't believe it, I was thinking as I mounted Dessie. The most famous horse in the world at the moment and I'm riding him!

He was huge and really powerful, and 'Dessie spotters'

139

would come from all over just to catch sight of him on the moors. We were approaching the top of a hill when about six or seven people suddenly appeared. 'Look, that's Dessie!' someone called out, and they started taking photographs. Richard smiled at them as we rode off quickly up the hill before they startled the horses. They continued taking pictures of us from behind, and Richard joked that they hadn't realised there were two famous arses on their shots that day – as they hadn't recognised mine!

I loved hanging around with Clare again and it made a great change from the pressures of work to go to the races or just have girly fun. I was still supposedly with Geoff but we'd rarely spoken and seen each other even less often over the past few years. I'd almost stopped visiting London and had even rented out my flat. We hadn't actually said we'd split up, but we were leading such different lives that it was inevitable we would, I suppose. Geoff's career with Zodiac Mindwarp had nose-dived. Music had changed and Kylie Minogue was what people wanted now. And while he was pleased that I was on the way up – there was no animosity – it just became clear that we had grown apart.

One day at the races with Clare, I met David Craig, now a sports presenter for Sky Sports News, but formerly a jockeys' agent who had looked after Jason Weaver, Fergal Lynch and Alan Munro, so now I really was back in with the racing gang again. I would often spend time with David racing, riding or having lunch and we became close, though he was never a boyfriend, more of a good pal.

I'd also become really good mates with Tony Pitts, who played Archie in *Emmerdale*. Now, he really was a naughty boy and one of those people you either loved or hated – and I loved him but I was one of the few in the cast who did. Tony reminded me of the bad lads from the bands I'd hung out with when I was younger, always having a laugh or playing a joke on someone – and usually offending them at the same time! He used to wander round the *Emmerdale* green room looking for mischief. And, considering you'd have show veterans like Sheila Mercier, who played Annie Sugden, sitting around knitting or reading a book, it must have been pretty awful when Tony would walk over to her, pretend to drop something and then bend over to fart in her face. He was always up for jokes and told it how it was – brutally honest, was our Tony – which, in the artificial setting of a television studio, I found refreshing.

Every Tuesday night, he would come over to my house and we'd tape *Vic Reeves' Big Night Out*, go to the pub, get hammered, argue about politics and religion with the locals, then stagger home, watch the video and go to bed – separately. Then we'd get up and go to work hungover – and we did exactly the same week after week.

We were a lucky bunch on *Emmerdale*, because it was quite a small cast of about 15, so we really were like a family, with its older generation and its younger ones. The *Emmerdale* kids – I was one of them – just! – soon became the Woolpack brat pack. Somehow, we all managed to rub along nicely; most of the time anyway.

One day, out of the blue, Mark Shaw from the band Then Jericho called. I'd bumped into him in London about a year after I'd joined the show and we'd swapped numbers, so when he called saying he'd like to come and see me I thought it might be a laugh. I'd known Mark on and off for years, having first met him when I was living in Charlotte Street and he was living down the road with Andy Taylor from Duran Duran. We used to hang out at the Embassy, where he did a bit of waitering. I'd liked him then but there were too many drugs going round in his crowd for me to want to be with him. But maybe that had all changed. Anyway, always a sucker for a pretty face and a leather jacket, I invited him to stay with me in Yorkshire for a couple of days.

I don't know how, but that weekend we ended up 'together' and suddenly one weekend turned into months and before I knew it he was with me full-time. Now, I'd always liked Mark, whose *Big Area* album was doing well in the charts, but I didn't want to marry him. In fact, I'd recently decided I didn't want to marry anyone. All the same, I was still drawn to him and had enjoyed the wildness and spontaneity of our relationship. I never could resist a bad boy, which was odd, as I'd also started finding myself strangely attracted to Peter Amory, who played my screen stepson. Peter was different from anyone I'd previously found attractive. He was grounded, professional and mature – a real man, not an immature dreamer like others I knew. But, since he was with someone else, I'd ignored those feelings and lurched on with Mark, despite still not actually having finished with Geoff.

Now Mark, despite doing well for himself, was always a bit tight with his money – something I've never found attractive – and definitely enjoyed the fact that I was now a 'bit famous'. My parents, who normally gave everyone a chance, didn't like him at all. After meeting him with me one Christmas at Piers's home, they said there was just something about him they didn't trust and even asked me never to invite him to their own house. I argued that they needed to give him a chance but I should have saved my breath because the following week he'd sold a story to the papers about 'our love', sealing his fate as a no-hoper in my parents' books. I wasn't pleased either, because I now had to get on the phone to Geoff – and pretty damn quick.

I told him everything. He surprised me by being really cool about it – he'd obviously been busy himself! – and our relationship, which had effectively ended over a year earlier, became a pure friendship, and we're still friends to this day. However, he did say I could do much better for myself but I defended Mark once again and put Geoff's and my parents' 'concerns' to the back of my mind when Mark surprised me by announcing that he was taking me on holiday. 'See,' I told Mum, 'he's not all bad.'

We had a lovely time in Spain, just having fun and chilling out, and I was beginning to remember again why I liked Mark. Then one night, when we were absolutely hammered on whisky, he pulled a ring out of his pocket (with a pearl in it – no diamond, the tight wad!) and proposed. Well, I was so drunk and caught up in the moment that I said yes, before we fell asleep laughing about it. But, as soon as I woke up in the morning, with a hangover from hell, I told Mark it was too soon and we should wait. With no intention of marrying him, in the cold light of day I was already plotting my escape. Mark seemed really adamant that it was a really good idea and we should get married really quickly, but I began to wonder if maybe he wanted to marry the soap star Claire King and not the real me.

We split up as soon as the plane had touched down back in England. A blast from the past had been fun, but I'd definitely grown up and now wanted to be with someone more reliable. After I dumped Mark, I didn't keep in touch. It was time to move on.

Bob Geldof, with the mighty Boomtown Rats.

*Above*: The TVR Taimar that Geldof disliked so much!

*Below*: With my partner in crime Fiona McKie.

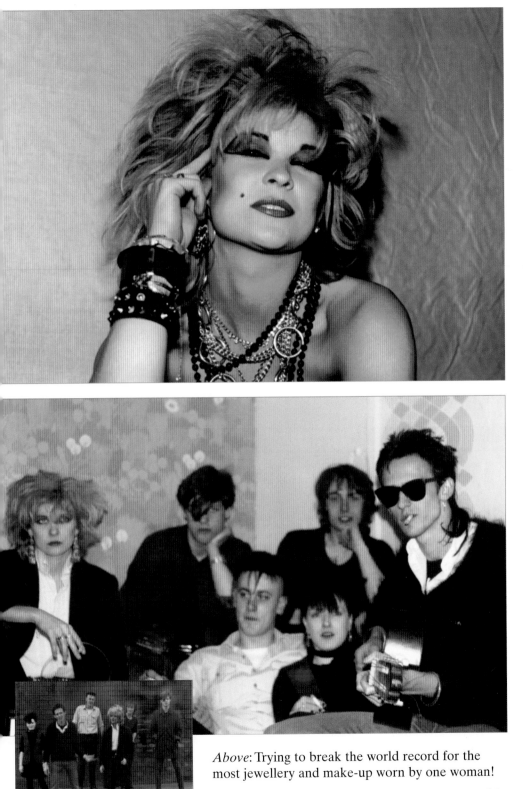

*Above*: Trying to break the world record for the most jewellery and make-up worn by one woman!

*Below and inset*: To Be Continued … that's me with the orange hair on the left of the main picture, and Stevie on the right.

*Above*: Our charity bash at Annabella's nightclub – me, Des Roche, Caroline Peach (née Prince) and Mark.

*Below left*: One of my favourite 1982 outfits.

*Below right*: London calling! With my Kawasaki 750cc, outside my flat in Camden Town.

*Above*: With Geoff Bird and Piers, relaxing at Roseberry Cottage.

*Below left*: Mark Shaw – a pretty face, but it wasn't enough for a lasting relationship!

*Below right*: The lovely Vinnie Jones – an entertaining encounter, to say the least!

*Above left*: The Kim Tate who arrived in *Emmerdale* was, surprisingly, quite a nice character... but not for long!

*Above right*: One of the criteria for playing Kim was to be able to ride – so I didn't have to lie on my application form!

*Below*: My screen family – Frank, Chris and Zoe Tate. I think we should have had a word with wardrobe about our jumpers!

*bove*: Kim Tate and Joe Sugden out hunting. We jumped a six-foot fence with a large rop on the other side – no health and safety to the rescue that day!

*elow*: Gorgeous Frankie Dettori. There was an instant spark between us when we met.

Kim and Karen's dramatic storylines guaranteed I often made an appearance on the front cover of many TV magazines.

# 13
# Boys to Men

**M**y disastrous episode with Mark behind me, I threw myself back into work, which was probably for the best, because the shooting days were increasing all the time as the Tates became more and more involved in the storylines. After about three months of solid slog and no social life, Tony Pitts came over to me in the green room one day and said, 'I've fixed you up on a date.' I tried to protest but he said I'd been working too hard and needed some fun, and he had just the man in mind.

'Who?' I said, vaguely interested; he was right – I could do with a bit of fun.

'Well, he's a mate of mine who plays for Leeds United and he's really into you. He watches the show and he wants to meet you.'

'Oh, OK then,' I said, thinking it might be fun after all.

'Great. His name's Vinnie Jones and I've given him

your address. He'll be round at 8pm,' Tony said, walking off laughing.

Trust Tony – giving out my address! What if I'd said no? He'd have turned up anyway! But I couldn't get annoyed, as he was trying to do me a favour really. As soon as I heard the name Vinnie Jones, I immediately knew who he was because he had quite a reputation in the tabloids for being football's bad boy. And, although he was a bit young for me, I thought, I'm single, so what the hell!

I'd recently moved into my brother's beautiful stone cottage in the heart of the village of Burton Leonard. His wife had recently sold the cottage I'd been renting since I'd moved back. The only down side to the property was that right opposite my bedroom window was a bottle bank, which wasn't much fun on a Sunday morning when all the local recyclers did their bit and disturbed my peace.

As Tony hadn't given me Vinnie's number, I couldn't contact him to find out where we'd be going. All I knew was, he was coming over to take me out at 8pm, so I wore a simple black dress and heels. I had to go to a charity auction with Stan Richards first and I thought this outfit would double up and be perfect for dinner or a club.

I arrived home at 8.15 to find Vinnie leaning on his car outside the house. 'All right, girl. How you doing?' he said as he opened the boot of his silver Merc, pulled out a case of beer and walked straight past me and up to the house. I was quite surprised at his attitude, but slightly turned on, as he was very confident for a lad in his early twenties. I opened the door and watched as he walked straight in, switched on the TV, kicked off his shoes, flopped on the sofa, opened a can of lager and started watching the football. I couldn't quite believe it. We're obviously not going out for dinner, then! I thought. I should have been angry but there was definitely something about him – which millions went on to witness when he appeared in the hit film *Lock, Stock and Two Smoking Barrels.*

'Wouldn't you rather have a glass of champagne?' I said as I opened a bottle for myself.

'Nah, darlin', this'll do me,' he answered. 'Now sit yer arse down and we'll watch the football.'

I laughed as I sat next to him. What else was a girl to do? Might as well run with it, I thought. Before long, as we got more and more drunk, we were having a really good laugh. And by the end of the match I'd drunk nearly two whole bottles of champagne and he'd nearly done the whole case of lager, so, when he flicked off the sound – what a gent! – and lunged at me, I didn't put up much resistance as he carried me upstairs. By now, I could hardly stand up, let alone say no!

The exact details of what followed have escaped me. I honestly can't remember much other than it being a bit of rough and tumble and quite good fun. Vinnie seemed to have a lot of energy and the case of lager hadn't dampened his, shall we say, spirits. Apparently, we had 'a right good sesh', or so he told me in the morning, but I had to take his word for it, as my mind was still awash with champagne. It was just one of those nights when two single people have fun, but he was a bit too laddish to consider seeing again.

After he left that morning – 'See ya, gal' – I had to go to work with a thumping head. I was a bit embarrassed at what I'd done. I hadn't intended to sleep with him and here I was not even able to remember the details of what we'd got up to. Yet it wasn't long before I was to up to naughtiness with another 'toy boy'.

When I wasn't filming, I was still hanging around with David Craig. One weekend he took me to Newmarket, where I was introduced to Matty Cowing, another jockeys' agent, who has since died and was such a lovely man. David then drove us over to the house of a little-known but up-and-coming jockey.

When Frankie Dettori opened the door and let us in, there was an instant spark between us. I thought he was stunning – at 19, very young, but utterly gorgeous. We sat in the living room having drinks and couldn't take our eyes off each other. I was telling myself, Claire, pull yourself together – he's far too young for you, but all such thoughts went out of my head when Frankie's hand brushed mine as he passed me a glass. It was obvious from his gestures that he thought I was David's girlfriend. I let him know subtly that I wasn't and, once it became obvious that we were both single, he started flirting outrageously, which made me fancy him even more – so young but so confident.

Friends of mine have often laughed over the years that I find certain jockeys attractive. Of course, they're on the small side, but they are so fit and the talent is often really attractive, so the height issue has never bothered me – and it didn't bother me with Frankie.

The four of us went in Matty's car to the Plough, near Newmarket, at the time a very trendy place to eat. With all the laughter and conversation, the energy flowing between me and Frankie across the dinner table was electric and continued all night.

On the way back, Matty and David sat in the front of the car and Frankie and I in the back. Not long into the drive, Frankie turned to me and started kissing me passionately. I tried to resist but couldn't help kissing him back. The boys noticed – I could see nudging and winking going on in the front – but I was past caring!

Once back at Frankie's house, where we were staying, David, who had not commented on what was going on and was quite drunk anyway, crashed out on the sofa. (This was an improvement on the time we'd stayed at the home of Matty and his lovely wife Rita, when he'd had to sleep on a lilo.) As Frankie led me away by the hand, I didn't hesitate. It didn't feel cheap – it just felt right. We were both single and I had no one to answer to but myself, so I followed him to his bed.

That night was amazing – and he was amazing! He might have been young but he certainly seemed to know what he was doing and he kept me up most of the night. We finally fell asleep around 3.30am, but at six he had to be up for 'riding out', so he kissed me goodbye and told me to sleep on. He looked so cute at the door when he turned and said in his funny English, 'I see you later, Claire.'

A few hours later, he woke me up with a boiled egg, which was breakfast to him, as jockeys hardly eat anything, and we had a laugh while I dunked my soldiers. From the start, we'd got on really well, so we swapped numbers and planned to meet again soon. I saw him the next week and, from then on, whenever he came up north to ride he would call me and we'd meet. We'd always go out for dinner and then back to my house for the night, although sometimes we'd splurge on a hotel. One time we made so much mess, thanks to a drunken food fight and a flooded bathroom, that Frankie had to pay the hotel a £500 cleaning bill. A stuffy couple we weren't!

We saw each other like this on and off for about two years and, although it wasn't that serious for either of us, as we were both very busy with our careers, we really liked each other.

One night, Frankie surprised me by turning up at my place unannounced. Normally this would have been great, but I'd promised to take Clare and my mum to see the Chippendales at Harrogate Conference Centre, and as Clare was due to return to the States soon I wanted to spend some time with her. So I told Frankie to amuse himself while I was out and promised to get back as soon as I could.

All the way to the show, Mum protested that we weren't to try to get her too 'involved', but after a few drinks she ended up having her photo taken with the oiled-up, near-naked strippers. I just couldn't get her out of there! After we'd prised her away and enjoyed a meal at our regular haunt, Gianni's, I realised how late it was, so I got a taxi for Mum and Clare and rushed home to Frankie.

It was all quiet downstairs as I let myself in, so I called out, 'Frankie! You here?' When there was no answer, I went upstairs, to be greeted by the sight of a very, very drunk Frankie, passed out on my bed with an empty bottle of wine next to him, a bottle of champagne in a chiller, rose petals scattered over the sheets and candles around the bed. It was just as well I got home when I did, as the candles had melted while he was asleep, oozing all over the side cabinet and on to the carpet, and were about to burn the house down!

Bless him, I thought, not a bit annoyed, as I poured water over the mess and took in the devastation in front of me. I woke him up and we had what was to be one of our last nights together. Even now, I know there was no reason other than work that caused us eventually to stop seeing each other. *Emmerdale* had become even busier for me, as Kim was really taking off with the audience and I was in more and more scenes. And, as for Frankie, he was quickly becoming one of the most successful young jockeys around, so we'd still see each other occasionally but our relationship was definitely winding down.

Back at work, I'd started spending more time on set with Peter Amory, who played Chris Tate. Kim was getting really popular and was in even more scenes. Chris was often in them with her and, because we were on set together alone a lot, we began to talk more than we had before. Peter confided in me that he was having difficulty in his relationship with his girlfriend, Sarah. She was unhappy living in Yorkshire and wanted to return to London, but Peter didn't. In turn, I told him how I'd become unhappy about not meeting a man who could look after me or with whom I could at least be on an equal footing. We talked about our personal lives and realised that neither of us was that happy with our current lot.

There was absolutely nothing more than that between us during that period, but, as we grew closer, the feelings I'd started to have for him while I was dating Mark resurfaced. But Peter was taken – wasn't he?

# 14

# Trial by Error

Clare, who'd moved to Santa Anita in California to work, had invited me out for a break. I didn't know it, but Frankie was already out there riding, so we ended up spending a lovely unplanned week together in the guesthouse on Clare's lot. The days flew by and I had a great time catching up with my old friend and really enjoyed being with Frankie. I hadn't seen him for quite a while, but I knew it would be the last time in that way because, among other things, it was becoming increasingly clear to me that my feelings for Peter Amory were not going away and I'd recently started to believe that he was beginning to feel the same way. There was something about the way we clicked on set. I could just feel it and I knew he could too. But, because Pete was still with Sarah, we continued to act together daily and simply ignored what seemed like an electric current flowing between us.

Even if he'd been free, I was in no rush to jump into another relationship that might not work out; this time I wanted it to be for real. But, because I knew he wasn't free, as soon as we'd finished our scenes I'd try to avoid him around the studios. I didn't want to let my feelings out and would never knowingly try to start a relationship with another woman's partner. The situation with Geldof and Paula had been completely different. I'd been just a teenager at the start and I broke it off as soon as it became totally clear that they were not going to split up.

I continued to avoid spending too much time with Pete, but each year the *Emmerdale* cast did a big weekend for charity in Blackpool and, as I'd always gone before, I couldn't suddenly say I wasn't going this time without it looking odd. I just hoped our rooms would be on opposite sides of the hotel.

These charity events were always crazy. This time, I started the day by being picked up in a helicopter and sandwiched between page-three legend Linda Lusardi, comedian Bobby Davro and the singer Linda Nolan, who was starring at Maggie May's on the pier. As well as me, Tony Pitts, Leah Bracknell, the McKays, Pete and Malandra Burrows had been invited. So there we all were, flying to the Vegas of the North and its infamous Golden Mile. All the girls were wearing brightly coloured jumpsuits and stilettos. The two Lindas' heels were so high I couldn't believe they could walk in them, let alone jump out of the helicopter for the photo shoot. And there was me in my jeans and boots – Mrs Unglamorous!

I didn't spend much time with Malandra Burrows on these trips; she always seemed to be a bit of a closed book to me, and never seemed to open up – well, not when I was around anyway. She often seemed to be in showbiz 'meet and greet' mode. Despite that fact that we filmed a lot of scenes together over the first few years of my being in the show, I never felt we really got beyond knowing each other more than we did that first day on set. She never really spoke to me about her personal life either – the complete opposite of her character, Kathy, who was never without a man!

After the photo calls, games and autograph signings, we headed back to the hotel to check in. Luckily, I was in a room next to Tony – or unluckily, if he was going to have one of his impromptu parties and I was trying to sleep. Anyway, we ended up hanging out together. One night when the two of us had been out drinking, he suddenly suggested we go for a swim in the sea. Thinking he was joking, I said, 'All right, as long as you go first.' That was a big mistake. Before I had a chance to stop him, he'd legged it on to the pier and plunged into the sea! The tide was in and the swells could have killed him, but with me screaming at him to come back he managed to drag himself out of the water. My heart was in my mouth until he was safe and sound and I made a mental note never to call his bluff again.

He soon sobered up, though, when he had to squelch through the hotel lobby soaking wet. I took him up to his room and told him to get dry.

Pete and I continued being 'just friends' and after another boozy night it was time to return to home and to work. Little did I know that booze was about to get me into masses of trouble but also bring Pete and I together.

Most afternoons during filming, we'd go into the pub next to the studio, the Fleece. Everyone went in those days – Stan, Pete, Peter Wren, Tony, Glenda and Moley (Malcolm Hamilton) – and it was nice just to get away from the studio for an hour. One day, we went in at lunchtime and because I wasn't due back on set until 3.30pm I had a couple of vodkas over a long lunch, assuming that, since I wouldn't be driving until much later and had eaten, I'd be fine. I ended up drinking doubles – someone else had got the drinks in – but I wasn't to know this until later.

Having finished filming later that evening, I set off to meet Shanti for dinner. During the meal, I had two glasses of wine, and I thought, I've had two drinks at lunchtime, eaten twice and several hours have passed in between, so I'm OK to drive. I was wrong.

After dropping Shanti at her home, I noticed a police car following me. As I turned round on a lane, they flashed at me to stop, which I did, and one of the officers came up to the window. 'Hello, Ms King, how's life on the farm?' he said, smiling. I laughed, assuming he was about to ask for my autograph, but suddenly he pulled out a breathalyser and said, 'Right, breathe into this.'

I wasn't worried. I thought I was within my limits and was quite annoyed to think that they'd pulled me just because they knew who I was.

I blew into the machine and was just about to give them a ticking-off when a positive reading flashed up. My mouth went dry. I just couldn't believe it. The officer ordered me out of the car, as I tried to explain that I hadn't been aware of being over the limit. Before I could say anything else, he snatched the keys from my hand, locked my car and bundled me into the back of the squad car. My heart was in my mouth as they took me to the police station, ribbing me, 'You're not lady of the manor now, are you?'

At the station, I was breathalysed again and shown to be just over the limit. I could see there was no point in trying to explain that I'd made a terrible but *accidental* mistake. I was formally arrested, then locked in a stinking cell for the night.

As I sat in the cold and dark, I read the walls, which were full of the scrawls of previous occupants. I really couldn't believe I was there. I pleaded for someone to let me make a call but it was hopeless. I kept crying and shouting for the officer to breathalyse me again. I was sure I was so little over the limit it would have cleared by now and then they could have simply charged me and let me go. My pleas went unanswered until hours later, when I was allowed my phone call and rang my brother. Piers arrived later but I wasn't to be let out for another six hours.

Eventually, I was given another breath test and found to be clear and told I could go. It was now 7am. After being handed a bail sheet – God, I was now a criminal – I was let out. Since Piers had left some hours earlier, I had to take a taxi to my car and once I'd driven home, already in a panic, I was confronted outside my door by about a dozen reporters and photographers, blocking my way.

My heart sank and I knew the only way the papers could have known was if the police had tipped them off. I had to fight my way through the hacks, who were asking me, 'Will you be sacked?' God, I hoped not. That hadn't entered my head until now, and as soon as I got inside I called the studio. I knew I had to talk to them before anyone else did. By this time, I was terrified that the reporters might have been right about my job.

The producer, Morag Bain, with whom I'd never really clicked, answered and I thought, Shit! She's going to sack me. But she surprised me by being quite nice and suggested I ring Keith Richardson, the executive producer. Keith had always been firm but fair and I hoped he'd understand I would never have caused trouble like this intentionally. Luckily, he stayed really calm and told me, 'We'll get round this. Just sit tight and we'll wait it out.' I felt a great weight lift. At least I won't lose my job but I'll still have to go to court, I thought, as the hacks screamed through my letterbox. That was one day I definitely didn't enjoy being famous.

My case was heard in February 1992 at Leeds Crown Court, where, after a brief hearing, I was fined £1,000 and banned from driving for 14 months. I was relieved it was over and just wanted to move on and forget it. Yes, I'd made a mistake but I hadn't killed anyone. My parents were furious with me but they couldn't say much, as my brother had lost his licence ten years earlier and his case had ended up in the papers too, though not for the same reason.

One night, he'd been at a barbecue and they'd all been drinking and having a laugh. He had drunk plenty, as he was planning to stay the night, but when he got pushed in the swimming pool he decided to drive home to get changed. The cold water seemed to sober him up, so he completely forgot he was over the limit. To make matters worse, because his clothes were soaked, he attempted to drive the short distance naked. Unfortunately, two minutes from home he was stopped by the police and arrested.

That time, too, the police tipped off the press and it made our local paper, the *Harrogate Advertiser*, with the headline 'Drunk driver caught with pants down!' How I laughed at the time, although now I was beginning to realise it wasn't so funny after all. It might sound as if I took the whole situation far too lightly, but I can assure you I didn't. I genuinely didn't believe I was over the limit, and, even if I was, I was certainly fit to drive. But I now know I shouldn't have chanced it. Luckily, no one was hurt.

We all learn our lessons and I learned that one the hard way. I did the crime, paid the fine and put it behind me.

# 15

# Love Actually

Strangely enough, it was the driving ban that brought Peter and I closer together.

Because we both played Tates, a lot of our call times were the same, and Pete, who lived not far from me, kindly offered to pick me up on his way to the studios. After the stress of losing my licence, I was more than grateful for his kind offer and on those many dark morning drives we got to know each other a lot better.

He told me how he and Sarah had been having problems and had planned to split up when they discovered she was pregnant. For the baby's sake, they'd given it another go, but now, two years on, both realised it still wasn't working. Their son Thomas was a toddler at the time and I remember feeling genuinely sad for them all that it hadn't worked out. No one wants to encourage a broken home, but it was clear that this home was already broken.

Following on from the lifts to and from work, we'd now started going out for dinner, once a week, then twice, then whenever we could. Nothing physical had happened between us – we just really enjoyed each other's company and constantly found we were last to leave the restaurant. We always chose small places because we didn't want to be spotted and have people assume we were having an affair when we weren't. We were also careful not to be photographed together by the paparazzi, as we certainly didn't want the press to blow it all out of proportion, and they were after me much more now because of the driving ban.

As much as I felt Pete wanted to be with me, just as I wanted to be with him, I was determined that nothing should happen between us unless he was single; nor would I encourage him to leave the relationship he was in, even though he seemed not to want to be there. We carried on like this for some while, spending time together and talking about everything except our obvious desire for each other. We seemed to have so much to chat about, including our record collections, which turned out to be very similar, as Pete had been a punk too.

Pete's habit of bringing me into the studios and waiting for me at the end of the day had already got people talking at work but I wanted to keep our growing friendship as quiet as possible, as it was really no one else's business and I still had no idea if it was going to lead to anything. My being drawn to him had taken me by surprise to begin with because, even though he was clearly attractive, he was not someone I would normally have gone 'Wow!' over. But he just had something about him.

I particularly loved the way he could command attention – a bit like my father – and hold an audience when he told his 'stories'. He could take the limelight away from me without trying, and I really liked that, because although I'm an actress I don't handle being the focus of attention too well. Mmm, I thought, as I watched him in full flow, that's my sort of man. I just wished he was *mine*.

One day on set, he took me to one side and told me that Sarah had given him an ultimatum: they either moved south or split up. Pete said he felt torn but he didn't want to go. Apart from anything else, he was filming here in Yorkshire, so it would be a logistical nightmare. But he also knew that, if he chose not to go, Sarah would be taking their son with her; this he understood, but he was really upset about the idea of not seeing Thomas every day. He ended by telling me that he'd decided to stay, so his relationship with Sarah was over. I should have been pleased that he was now single, but over the next few weeks it broke my heart to see him in pieces. He missed Thomas dreadfully but felt it was right that he was with his mum.

During the following weeks and months, we spent even more time together, and now he had no one to go home for. Both of us knew we were fighting our feelings but neither of us acted on them. I tried to comfort Pete and we continued going out but nothing actually happened between us until Sarah told him that she had a new man and he'd moved in with her. This seemed to give Pete the push he needed to take things further with me, and, boy, was I ready.

It was coming up for Christmas and one afternoon on set Pete asked me what I was going to do for the break. I told him I was planning to go to Barbados. I'd taken my parents the year before and had met Trish and Robin Bradford, who lived there and not only ensured we had a really great holiday but invited me to come back any time. Pete looked me deep in the eyes and said, 'I was going to Africa but...' I finished his sentence for him: 'But now you're coming with me.' He smiled and the next week we flew away, as a couple.

The waiting was over, although I wasn't going to tell anyone yet just in case it didn't work out. I needn't have worried, though, as we spent the whole two weeks laughing, making love and getting to know each other even better. We found we liked the same things; he liked his racing and, as everyone knows, so do I. It was perfect and we flew back united.

I was in love, and this time it felt different, it felt grounded, real, for keeps – I hoped.

Almost as soon as I was back home – Pete had dropped me off – the phone rang. 'My girlfriend's mother has just been sat two seats behind you and Pete on a flight back from Barbados – and apparently you looked very cosy,' said my mate Mark Styles.

I laughed and admitted that we'd just started seeing each other. I didn't deny it as we had nothing to hide and Mark was a good friend. But, considering Mark's girlfriend was Glenda McKay from *Emmerdale*, I knew that by now everyone else must know.

I called and warned Pete, who just laughed, saying, 'Well then, that means we're definitely going to go for it then, doesn't it?'

I smiled – not that he could see me. He made me smile a lot in those days. 'Yes,' I said. 'It does.'

I floated back to work a couple of days later, on top of the world. Everything was going so well. I've a got lovely boyfriend and I love my job, I thought. I was walking down the corridor at Yorkshire Television when I smiled at the receptionist, who looked rather glum. 'What's up?' I asked.

'Oh, you won't have heard, will you, as you've been away,' she replied.

My happy mood suddenly grew a little greyer. 'What?' I said, praying it was nothing directly to do with me. It suddenly reminded me of the early days, when I seemed to have landed on my feet acting-wise but often felt like one day someone would notice I was blagging it and pull the rug from under me. She explained that all the cast and crew had been called to a meeting to announce that Phil Redmond, of *Brookside* fame, was coming to 'shake the show up'. The cast had been told to expect 'massive changes'. Now, in soapland 'massive changes' normally means one thing – deaths. I thanked her for telling me and rushed off to get ready to go on set.

No point in panicking just yet, I told myself, as I

struggled to put Kim's left stiletto on my right foot for the second time. And just when everything was going perfectly, I thought, as I made my way to the green room. The atmosphere was one I'd never known on the show – panic had definitely set in. Everyone I met could speak of nothing else, and whispers about who might be axed filled the sets and dressing rooms. Overnight, they'd gone from a bunch of happy campers to a gang of edgy worriers.

Even before I'd learned whether or not I'd be safe from the axe, I wasn't that worried about Phil Redmond joining the show. Actually, I thought it could be just what we needed. Although the show was popular, it wasn't getting the recognition it deserved, but of course I never told anyone that at the time. I watched *Brookside* and was a big fan of what Redmond had done there; he'd been really pushing the soap boundaries with the 'Jordache body under the patio' storyline and was well known for his shocking story directions. I was secretly hoping for something like that. As far as I was concerned, Kim would gladly have buried Frank in the gardens of Home Farm!

On the day of the 'big meeting' we were all called into the canteen – hardly glamorous, it seemed more rag trade than showbiz. A few drinks and nibbles were provided but I don't remember anyone eating. Drinking, yes! One by one, the nervous cast members took their seats, then suddenly Phil walked in and introduced himself in his strong Scouse accent and said, 'Right – I've been brought in to shake things up. I'm going to have a bit of a change-round and there's going to be a plane crash, but you won't know what's happening until you get your scripts – so until then enjoy yourselves.' With that, he walked out smiling. Subtle he wasn't! And the prospect of waiting now made things even worse.

Over the next few weeks, the cast seemed to be up in arms about Redmond's arrival, especially the older members. What's he doing coming over from *that sort of show* to this one? was the general cry. Pete wasn't sure what to make of him either, because we knew there were going to be deaths in the crash, all you could hear everywhere you went was: 'Who's going to go?' and 'Is it me?' Everyone, myself included, seemed to think it was them, and it could have been anyone, because with soaps that's the nature of the beast. You're only as good as your contract and when that's up it's up. If you think you're there forever, you'll be in for a short, sharp shock when you're told you're not. I kept telling myself that I'd had a good run and it wouldn't be the end of the world if Kim was axed. Kidding myself, I think is the word.

The plane crash was supposed to be shot at the end of the summer, but for some reason they fell behind with the planning and it was November before we started filming that block of storylines. Not a major problem, but it would make the already arduous outdoor shoots much harder for some people than it should have been. Once we'd received the scripts, we knew who was going and who was staying. I was relieved to see that I had been saved, as I was in the batch of scripts that followed the crash, but I felt sick when the executive producer, Keith

Richardson, called Pete into his office. I hugged Pete, who was sure he was about to be axed, and I waited outside the office, my stomach knotted with worry. I didn't want to lose him now and I didn't think the character deserved to go either. Inside the office, Keith sat him down and said, 'We've decided that one of the main characters is going to be disabled by the accident and will end up in a wheelchair.'

'We've discussed it several times,' Keith continued, 'and we think you're the only one strong enough to carry it off. You're the best actor for the job, Pete. How do you feel about it happening to Chris?'

'How long is it for?' Pete asked.

'We're not sure yet – but we think it might be permanent,' Keith replied. It was really good of Keith to be so honest, as they could have easily lied at this stage.

Pete thought about it for a moment and said, 'Right, well, it's a challenge – so let's go for it.'

Once he told me he was staying, I was thrilled but didn't envy what lay in store for him. Pete knew my dad was now in a wheelchair with multiple sclerosis, so he used him for research and Dad was more than pleased to help.

They were right to choose Pete, as he was the only one who could carry it off, and he went on to do an amazing job.

In November, we started filming from 4pm until 3am in the *Emmerdale* lanes and outdoor sets. It was freezing cold and the weather was constantly miserable. I think it rained nearly every day and no one was feeling particularly cheery. The lovely make-up ladies took pity on us all and decided it would be a morale booster if we had champagne cocktails before we started each day, so they used to have them ready for us for when we'd come out of make-up. It was the little things like that that gave you the drive to get back out there during what was a pretty harrowing time.

As fake dead bodies fell from the sky, the sets were destroyed, and some of the cast could be found in corners of the green room worrying that 'the audience won't go for it' and fearing it would ruin the show. Phil Redmond had 'gone too far this time,' they muttered. Poor Pete really did suffer for his art; trapped underneath the collapsed Woolpack for nights and nights in the pouring rain. He would later describe the doomed pub as his early grave!

It really was a hard slog. Lots of problems arose with the special effects: pyrotechnics kept exploding when they shouldn't have and there were quite a few near-death experiences before the shoot was over. But in the end I think we all knew the stuntmen and SFX people had done a brilliant job. When we finally saw the preview tapes, I knew that life on *Emmerdale Farm* had changed forever.

Phil Redmond's new direction really did change the show for the better. Although there were casualties – the most upsetting departure for me was that of Tony Pitts, which was awful – and there was inaccurate press criticism of apparent similarities between our storyline and the truly horrific Lockerbie disaster, which was really distressing, but Redmond's stint on the show proved a huge success. After 20 years, *Emmerdale* had finally arrived.

# 16

# Stalked

The show's change of profile following the revamp really brought Kim to the attention of the masses. Suddenly, *Emmerdale* was more successful than ever and almost overnight I was on the cover of practically every television guide, whereas we'd normally only featured inside. The interest from newspapers and magazines was over-whelming. People wanted to know all about me, my relationship with Pete – this had leaked out by now – my past, my present and even what I thought of the future! I was voted best bitch, best bum, sexiest female, most popular celebrity – it was crazy!

All this media attention stirred up mixed feelings in me. I tried to keep my private life as private as possible, knowing how difficult famous people seemed to find it conducting a relationship in a goldfish bowl. At the same time, I could see that it's a 50/50 relationship where backs have to be scratched if either side wants to get anywhere. A programme needs publicity and the media are the only ones who can give you it, so you have to take the risks.

With the show pulling in millions of viewers, we moved to the 7pm slot, so now we were 'primetime' and well and truly on the nation's radar. Having previously hardened Kim up, the writers decided to take her to new heights of 'evil', and she started to attract a title that is much used now but didn't exist until Kim Tate wreaked havoc across the Dales – 'Superbitch'.

I first became aware that Kim was *really* making an impact when out and about in my home town. For my first few years on *Emmerdale*, I'd always been pretty much left alone in Harrogate, but now local people had started asking for autographs everywhere I went in the area. I couldn't even use a pub toilet without someone wanting my signature as I was washing my hands! Although I didn't really mind this sort of attention, I did find it a bit odd. Suddenly, everyone wanted a piece of me, and I thought back to the days when I'd been the 'plus-one' because my partners had been more successful – and now here I was the invitee.

One day I was in M&S just minding my own business as I browsed through the wine section, when this little old lady walked towards me, looking a little overexcited and shaking an umbrella. I was just putting myself in fan-friendly mode as she reached me, but instead of asking for an autograph she started whacking me over the head with her umbrella, screaming that I was a bitch for treating

Frank badly. I managed to move out of the way, ditch my basket and leg it out of the shop. I'd wanted to hit her back but I knew that wouldn't look too good in the *Sun* – 'Soap star punches OAP!'

I wandered off, rubbing my head and feeling both annoyed and confused. I'm getting abused! Actually getting attacked! What on earth is happening? I'm only playing a part, for God's sake. I'm not actually Kim Tate – I'm Claire King, I thought. As I got in my car, little did I know that Kim was to evoke stronger and even stranger reactions than that old woman's.

I was still 'riding out' whenever I could, but less and less often since *Emmerdale* was becoming much more demanding of my time. By now, I'd ridden in five races and, you guessed it, won zip! But I didn't mind, as they were great fun and I normally did OK, although my 'poor ability' enabled me to pick up a seven-day ban at Doncaster Races – not one of my proudest moments!

Around this time, I met a Thirsk trainer called Les Eyre, who suggested I should run a syndicate. My profile was quite high by now and I was getting offers like this quite often, but I liked Les, so we set up the Claire King Partnership. We didn't do very well, but we went on to become firm friends and I still have a share of a horse with him, Creskeld, who's in Spain, where Les now trains, so at least something good came out of it.

As the audience figures continued to rise – they were now over ten million – the Tates were becoming *Emmerdale*'s 'love to hate' favourites. Viewers loved the antics and the rivalries that the family seemed to thrive on. Before the plane crash, I was getting a fair amount of fan letters each week, a couple of dozen or so, asking for signed photos, or nice ladies asking where I'd got a certain jacket or pair of shoes and so on. Then, all of a sudden, I was getting hundreds and hundreds. At work, it became a running joke that the postman fancied me, as he was in there so often. I bet he hated me, more like, for having to lug all those bags in each week!

Most of the letters were nice ones where fans had painted pictures of me or included little presents. Then there were the marriage proposals. And the begging letters – make your own money! One day, a letter came from a guy who wrote to say he was in the process of a sex change and that he had instructed the doctors to make him look just like me – well, Kim actually, although I suppose my face is my own. But now someone even wanted that! – and could he please have my vital statistics to make sure they got him 'just right'?

I got lots more letters from him, suggesting that once we were identical we could become lesbian lovers. Well, I've always thought I was OK-looking, but I've never fancied 'me' in that way – so I passed on that one!

It was becoming so bizarre, and I wasn't even safe at home. When my clothes started going missing from the washing line, it was scary to think anyone knew where I lived, but I just upped the security and got on with my life. The press was still going crazy for Kim and I was now doing about 30 front covers a year. Cartoon strips based on me appeared in the *Sun* and the *TV Times*. I actually loved them, which was apparently very rare, and even asked for a print. One artist, John Ireland, sent me a signed copy, which is still proudly displayed in my loo.

And then there were the soap awards. Several times, I was up against Michelle Collins, who played *EastEnders* bitch Cindy Beale, and later I was constantly pitted against Martine McCutcheon, who played the soap's Tiffany Mitchell, an incredibly popular character – so no chance of a doorstop for the loo there!

When I actually won 'Soap's Biggest Bitch' and 'Most Evil Woman', I did worry a bit that people were confusing the character with me, but then I said to myself, What the heck! Run with it, Claire. I knew Kim was a total one-off and that people seemed to love whatever she got up to, so I threw myself into playing up to the image that people expected and duly pitched up at the awards ceremonies, which were quite basic back then, and smiled while I picked up the honours for 'Best Bum'!

Pete moved in, partly because we wanted to take our relationship on to the next level but also because, with my high profile, I was feeling a bit vulnerable at home on my own. It was a good thing he did, because soon all sorts of odd things started to happen.

I would open the post and find letters patched together with pieces cut out from newspapers that read, 'We're gonna get you, bitch' or 'Who the fuck do you think you are, Claire?' or 'Enjoy it while you can as soon you'll be dead.' I felt physically sick when I opened these and thank

God Pete was at home to give me a reassuring cuddle. Pete pointed out that they had been posted from quite far away and said that whoever it was would probably stop now that they'd got it out of their system.

But the letters continued.

I could cope with letters that had been posted but when they started being delivered to my next-door neighbours, Sally and Jim, as handwritten notes, I was really scared. Whoever was doing this was lurking around outside my home – it was getting serious. Luckily, my neighbours were lovely and instantly knew that the notes – which said things like, 'Don't park outside my gateway again or I'll smash your windows in – from Claire' – were definitely not from me.

Not long after this, skips started being delivered to my drive, ordered in my name, cement was dumped outside, my car was scratched and one of my wheels was loosened. The handwritten notes to my neighbours continued.

I finally realised my 'stalker' wasn't fooling when the phone – my home number was ex-directory – started ringing late at night. It would ring around 1am and when I picked it up I would hear a tape recording of my own voice being played back to me. If I ignored the calls and let the machine pick it up, vile and weird messages would fill the tape, some threatening to 'put me in a ditch', others saying, 'I'm watching you.' Naturally, I was scared and mystified by this hate campaign that I was attracting, but, when I started getting silent calls on my private mobile, of which very few people had the number, I realised that it

All smiles on the day I became Mrs Walton. Peter and I both had to adopt stage names
as there was already both a Claire Seed and a Peter Walton in the business. We are
pictured here with Neil Morrissey.

*Above*: Celebrating with friends from the *Emmerdale* cast.
*From left to right*: Richard Thorp, Finnoula Ellwood,
Craig McKay, Pete, me, Stan Richards, Glenda McKay,
Clive Hornby and Tony Pitts.

*Below*: With family, bridesmaids Clare and Fiona and best
man Matt Stratford.

*Inset*: The last kiss Pete and I shared before we became
husband and wife. Despite everything that has happened,
this is still a treasured photograph and sits by my bed.

A publicity shot for the *Worth Coming Home Early For* campaign, which marked a change of pace for *Emmerdale*.

My storylines as Kim were often raunchy and intriguing – but never dull.

*Above*: Kim gets hot under the collar in the hay with Dave Glover. In the show, Dave and Kim had an affair that had the nation hooked.

*Below*: With Frank Tate filming the fire that killed Dave as he tried to rescue baby James

*above left*: The only time you'll ever see me in this state! Kim goes through the agony of childbirth.

*above right*: The shock of seeing Kim back from the dead was enough to give Frank a heart attack!

*below left*: Another of Kim's victims! Kim let husband Steve Marchant take the blame for a stolen stallion scam.

*below right*: Just before Kim left the show, she tipped Chris out of his wheelchair and hit him over the head with a bowling ball. She wasn't called a superbitch for nothing!

Kim and son James make their dramatic exit from *Emmerdale* … perhaps we will return in the not-too-distant future?

h the wonderful Desert Orchid at Fryup.

*Above*: Riding Fair Dare at Redcar when I was an amateur jockey.

*Below*: Mum and I out on the West of Yore hunt.

was possible I knew the person who was doing this to me.

The fear turned into anger – which helped, actually – and I racked my brains as to who it could be. I suddenly had a feeling that it was a woman and, after listening to the distorted voice on the tapes, I even thought I recognised the voice. But, as I wouldn't have been able to prove it without getting the police in to monitor the calls – which I simply didn't have the time to do, since my schedule was busier than ever, and in any case I didn't want to lose my privacy by having my phone tapped – I decided that I would take a chance on my hunch. So I called the woman, leaving a message saying in no uncertain terms that I knew it was her and I'd better not hear from her again or I'd call the police.

The calls stopped immediately. I won't name her in this book, as I never proved it was her, but we both know who she is.

# 17

# Married

After the hate campaign ended, Pete and I got on with enjoying life in the cottage I'd recently bought in Killinghall, just outside Harrogate. His son Thomas would visit us for weekends and we became one big happy family. It was lovely to have the house bursting with laughter and fun when Thomas was with us but it was also great just to be in front of the fire with Pete, sharing a bottle of wine and talking. I never got bored spending time with him; we had loads in common and because we worked together there was always something to talk about. I'd happily have been stranded on a desert island with him and a few cases of wine!

We just *clicked*, and you don't start to imagine spending the rest of your life with just one man if that man doesn't satisfy you in every way. I was well and truly smitten and happier than I'd ever been.

Almost two years to the day of the event in Blackpool, we were invited on the yearly charity trip again. As everyone knew we were together by now, this time we had the same room. And after doing all the usual photo calls and visiting the children's hospital, the cast went on a bar crawl around town and got absolutely hammered. Now, Pete and I could hold our drinks but this night we really were sozzled. We'd been invited to see Linda Nolan's show – she was back at Maggie May's – where we knocked back several more drinks, which we needed when Craig McKay (who played Mark Hughes in *Emmerdale*) murdered 'New York, New York' with her on stage!

About 2pm, we made our way back to the hotel and, after we'd staggered into our room laughing, Pete suddenly stopped laughing and turned to me. 'Claire,' he said, slurring.

'What?' I said, sitting down on the bed – well, falling actually.

'Will you... marry me?' he murmured, standing by the bed and looking down.

In shock, I pulled myself up and screamed, 'Yes! Yes! Yes!' – God knows what the people in the next room thought we were doing – and with that we kissed and passed out.

When we woke up the next morning, Pete looked at me oddly. I started to worry that because he'd been very drunk he might not have meant to propose and would try to make a joke of it.

'Oh, God! What happened last night?' I whispered.

Quick as a flash, Pete answered, 'I asked you to marry me – and you said yes.'

We both paused – to see if either of us still wanted to say we'd not said it. I smiled at him and he started laughing. It felt unreal to be having this conversation, as Pete and I were well known for saying we never wanted to get married. He held my hand and repeated that he really wanted to marry me. As the words came out of his mouth, my heart seemed to skip a beat. I know that sounds corny, but it really did! I told him that if he wanted me to marry him he'd have to propose properly.

At this, he laughed and got down on one knee, grimacing as the hangover kicked in. 'Would you do me the honour of being my wife?' he said, looking up at me with his gorgeous brown eyes.

I stared at him hard for a minute as moments from my romantic life seemed to flash before me, times I'd thought I was happy with others I'd been involved with. I was asking myself, Is he definitely the right person for me? But, for the first time in my life, I got an overwhelming feeling that *he* was the one person who wanted to be with me as much as I wanted to be with him. I realised in that very moment that he was the one man I wanted to share the rest of my life with. 'Yes, I would love to marry you,' I said, as Pete pulled me to him and we kissed. As we lay back on the bed, I said playfully, 'You do know you're going to have to ask my dad, don't you?'

He agreed nervously and we decided to keep the engagement to ourselves until the following weekend, when we would be with my parents at the local horse show at Ripley, a beautiful village and castle owned by my friends Sir Thomas and Lady Emma Ingleby. I told Pete to wait until we were back at their home afterwards before saying anything.

On the day of the show, we were all having a great time and I was on cloud nine with my secret. I couldn't wait to tell Mum and Dad the news later and they both remarked on my excellent mood. I was just walking by the members' tent when I spotted Frazer Hines's girlfriend, Liz Hobbs. I'd always said hello to her at awards or at the races, as she was Frazer's partner, so I waved at her across the paddock, but instead of waving back she just stared at me oddly. Strange, I thought. What's her problem? I was going to go over and see what was wrong, but I decided she must have just had a few too many drinks and ignored her, instead making my way back to Pete and my parents.

A few hours later, as we were about to leave, I heard someone shouting my name. I turned round to see a very drunk Liz barging her way through the crowds towards us – with Frazer in hot pursuit. I was wondering what on earth was wrong with her today, when she started screaming at the top of her voice that she knew I was having an affair with Frazer and she was going to tell everyone what I was really like. Well, I could have died! By now, everyone was staring at us. Mum and Dad looked at me quizzically and Pete looked confused, to say the least, as Liz launched into a tirade about a completely fictitious affair I was supposed to be having with her man.

I couldn't believe this was happening on my engagement day – no one knew yet, but *I* did, and today had been really special until she'd appeared. Here I was having ridiculous accusations thrown at me in front of my future husband and my parents, not to mention the crowd that had gathered. I was just about to tell Liz in no uncertain terms that she was barking up the wrong tree and that if she didn't get away from me right now I'd knock her block off, when Frazer, who had been apologising profusely throughout the whole episode, grabbed her by the arm and dragged her off. Luckily, everyone knew that there had never been anything between Frazer and me. 'Some tart's obviously left her earrings in his bed or shower and here I am getting the blame!' I said as we made our way through the crowds to leave the show. I was really upset, as it was supposed to be my special day and she'd ruined it. Years later, she apologised, but it was too late by then.

We drove back to my parents' house and, on the way, when I'd calmed down, Pete squeezed my hand and I felt better. I felt I wasn't alone any more and managed to focus on the good news we were about to spring on my parents.

Back at home, Mum said she'd get some drinks and I went to help her. As I exited the room, Pete looked at me as if to say, 'Oh no, you don't.' I shot back an 'Oh yes I do' look and left him to ask Dad if he could marry his daughter. I went through to the kitchen with Mum, saying, 'I think we'd better get the champagne out – because at this moment Pete's asking Dad for my hand in marriage.' Bless Mum, she started crying and hugged me, saying how pleased she was for us and that she really liked Pete. In fact, when we'd first got together, my parents had had reservations about him, because he already had a child, and a young one at that, but he soon won them round with his charms. He was nothing like Chris Tate, thank God!

After about ten minutes in the kitchen with Mum, I thought it had gone a bit too quiet in the living room, so I popped my ear round the door and heard Dad saying to Pete that, if he ever, ever hurt his daughter or did anything to upset me, he'd have a shotgun up his arse so fast he wouldn't know what was happening! Poor Pete's face was as white as a sheet. And all he kept saying was, 'No, sir, no, sir. I promise!' I wish he'd remembered that ten years later.

Once we knew the deed was done, Mum and I went in with drinks and we all toasted our engagement. I didn't have a ring yet; I wanted something special and fancied something old, rather than a standard shiny new ring, so we went to see my uncle Peter (Wilson), who dealt in antique jewellery. Pete bought me a stunning ring, a solitaire diamond set in platinum with three diamonds down each shoulder, and, even before it was on my finger, Mum had a notepad out and was jotting down ideas for the wedding.

'Right,' she said as she paced the room. 'Guest list, cars, dress, cake... Claire, we'll have to get a...'

I tuned out as the details weren't what interested me. I just wanted to marry the man I loved – everything else was gravy! I was aware, however, that a wedding befitting the very public image of the couple getting married was going to cost my parents a fair old whack, which worried me.

Luckily, Shanti, my press agent, said that if we did a deal with a magazine for the pictures they would help out with the cost of the wedding. I immediately thought that this might be a good idea, as I didn't want to land Dad with the whole cost, but I explained to her that she would have to be very clear with whoever she was dealing with that I didn't want some huge, over-the-top affair or a magazine editor dictating how my special day would be. Plus, Pete always loathed the press, so I knew he wouldn't want to be doing some 20-page special. Shanti understood my concerns and, after making a few calls, organised a deal with the *News of the World*'s supplement magazine. They would cover the cost of the wedding and honeymoon, as long as they had the full exclusive, but it would only be a few pages on one Sunday – not like today's *OK* and *Hello*, where it would run for two issues and 50 pages!

Pete was 100 per cent against it, but, as Dad was insistent that he wanted to pay for the wedding, we decided we'd go for it since it meant he didn't have to foot the whole bill.

It wasn't long before I realised I might have made a mistake accepting the deal, because suddenly I was being told what sort of dresses my bridesmaids should have and informed how many security guards would be needed. I was prepared for a bit of give and take – as they were paying for it – but when the magazine announced they wanted to approve my dress I rang Shanti and told her if they didn't back off I wanted out. She then made several frantic calls, only to have to tell me that, as the deal had already been signed, I just had to get on with it. But she said she'd told the magazine editor in no certain terms that, despite what anyone said, I was choosing my own dress.

I felt a bit better about it now, but I wouldn't agree to the 'before photos' that had suddenly been requested, and I stood firm, so they weren't happy. It also became clear that our wedding was going to end up being more for our families than for us. I only had enough room on the guest list for about a dozen of my own friends, which I know often happens, but I thought, Well, at least the ceremony will be just for us. That would be the nerve-racking bit – or so I thought.

Over the weeks coming up to the big day, I wobbled many times but, hoping I was doing the right thing, I somehow conquered my jitters and started the search for the perfect dress. In Harrogate, I'd seen a beautiful dress that had been made by a Shrewsbury-based designer called Hayley J. We drove down to see her and I was able to help design it. 'I've no intention of being your typical meringued-up bride,' I said to her as she got out her sketchpad, but she didn't blink when I told her I wanted to incorporate a riding hat and boots, so I knew I'd picked the right woman for the job. Later, the *Emmerdale* bosses copied my wedding dress for the remarriage to Frank – cheapskates!

Before long, it was the day of the rehearsal at Nidd

Church – which turned out to be a right disaster. My best friends, Fiona, who had come over from Greece, where she now lived with her husband, Nico, and Clare, who had flown in from the States, were with me, so I was really pleased to have my girls back. Even so, the day wasn't running as smoothly as I would have liked.

Clare and I had gone to have some last-minute alterations to the bridesmaids' dresses done and were on our way back, when we got stuck in thick traffic. I started to panic because we were already running late and still had to pick up Fiona for the rehearsal, knowing everyone else was already at the church. Fiona had called to say she was waiting for us in the local pub, and when we finally got there I dashed inside, only to find her totally smashed at the end of the bar! This is all I need! I thought, as I walked her, swaying, to the car.

I was just putting her in the back seat when Dad rang my mobile, shouting, 'Claire! I'm waiting by the aisle. Where the fuck are you?'

'Dad!' I said. 'You're in a bloody church – you can't swear! Just hang on – I'm on my way!'

I drove off at breakneck speed, as I knew Pete was waiting with his parents, Brian and Mollie, who'd travelled from New Zealand, and I didn't want them to worry. Everything seemed to be going wrong but never for one moment did I doubt that I wanted to marry Pete. I just needed to get to him! As soon as the traffic eased, I was on my way and, because we'd had the windows fully open, Fiona seemed to be sobering up.

When we screeched into the church car park, I saw Dad standing by the entrance, and that touched me so much I nearly burst into tears. It was a real effort for him to walk because he was suffering badly with MS by now and was pretty much wheelchair-bound, but he had been determined to walk me down the aisle, with the aid of what he called his 'drinks trolley' – a funky walking aid with wheels. Once out of the car and safely on his arm, we could at last get the rehearsal out of the way.

Clare, Fiona and I were staying at my parents' house, and the night before the wedding, desperate for a drink, we sneaked out to the local pub. I also knew a lot of the people who had come for the wedding would be there and I wanted to say hello to everyone. Pete was there too, propping up the bar and looking totally white with nerves. Noticing the lime and soda in front of him, I asked, 'Why aren't you drinking?' He said he'd been drinking soda and keeping his hand over his glass all night, so it couldn't be spiked, because he knew what his mates were like!

Pete bought us girls a bottle of wine and we all had a drink together. He said he was really looking forward to the honeymoon, so we could be alone. I told him not to worry, as our big day was going to be perfect. I didn't want to see him after midnight – call me superstitious! I was just about to head back home with the girls when someone said Pete and I should have a final picture taken together while we were still single. For the photo, he kissed me goodnight – our last kiss as singles. I love that picture and even now, after all that has happened, it's still in a frame by my bed.

That night, I lay awake worrying and hoping that everything would go well. I had no doubts at all about marrying Pete; I was more worried about the magazine's involvement! Eventually, I fell asleep and after what seemed like minutes it was the morning of 2 July 1994 and Shanti had arrived with my hairdresser and mate, Caroline, so it was time to start getting ready. Fiona kept asking my dad to open the champers but he wouldn't let us have a drink until we were ready, despite our pleas. He knew we would have got pissed!

The *News of the World* journalist turned up in a total state. She was barely through the front door when she started telling everyone all about the problems she was having with her editor and how the security wasn't right, as there were dozens of photographers from rival publications desperate to get photos of us on the way to the church. If any of these got pictures, all hell would break loose, she said.

Shanti kept her away from me, as I was nervous enough already and the last thing I wanted to hear right now was what was going wrong. She knew I'd already heard every word, but told me I wasn't to worry about what the reporter had said. Then she explained that the car coming to take me to the church, which was waiting only a few minutes' drive away, would have to cruise around for a while to kill time and avoid the paparazzi. I agreed and after a half-hour's delay we got in the car and set off for the short drive to the church.

We'd not been on the road a couple of minutes when

about 20 or 30 paparazzi descended on us and chased the car up the lane taking pictures. I was shocked and my dad got angry, but the *News of the World* girl topped it all by bursting into tears! We tried to ignore what was going on and headed for the church.

Dad, sitting next to me, looked more nervous than I did. 'I want you to know how proud I am of you,' he said. I hugged him and thanked him for being a brilliant dad. He laughed and made a joke about not being able to walk me all the way down the aisle. 'Just take your time,' I said and squeezed his hand.

We pulled up outside the church to find even more photographers, who needed us to pose for the official pictures, so while we were doing this everyone in the church thought I still hadn't arrived, and poor Pete was waiting nervously at the altar. We entered the church as 'The Bridal March' started. Dad practically dragged me down the aisle, rushing as fast as he could, thinking he wouldn't be able to make it the whole way. What an entrance – late and legging it to the altar!

Pete was staring at me from the moment I entered the church. Ronnie Kent, the vicar, had told him not to be shy and to stand boldly and proudly – which I thought was lovely advice. Ronnie, a deeply intelligent and particularly eloquent man, is sadly no longer with us.

Once I'd reached Pete, Ronnie told us to hold hands, and as I did so I noticed Pete's face was dripping with sweat. 'Are you all right? I mouthed.

'Yes – are you pissed?' he asked, and I laughed out loud.

We had two beautiful readings, one by Pete's mum, Mollie, and the other by Richard Thorp (Alan Turner from *Emmerdale*), then, as the vicar pronounced us married, the colour returned to Pete's cheeks and he kissed me.

As we left the church, there were press everywhere and, when several bodyguards came rushing in, sending people flying, pandemonium ensued. Pulling Mum to one side, I said, 'Get everyone over to the drinks and I'll do the pictures.' She nodded and went off to herd the hundreds of guests towards the champagne being served in the grounds. I wished I was going with her.

Pete and I got in the carriage for the short ride to the Nidd Hall Hotel. Just before setting off, we posed with gritted teeth for the shots, while the madness continued around us. Suddenly, a photographer appeared from nowhere, trying to jump inside the carriage to take pictures, but, quick as a flash, a burly security guard dragged him out. It was beyond crazy – no amount of money was worth this! We were just recovering when another photographer, who'd climbed a tree to get a shot with a telephoto lens, suddenly fell out of it and landed in front of us, almost causing the carriage to career off the road. He could have killed himself or all of us. Thank God, we had a good sense of humour, otherwise I'd have been crying on my wedding day.

The coach raced off and we soon arrived at the hotel – which was surrounded by guards – where we had to pose for yet more pictures! I felt so sorry for the guests who weren't allowed to take any photos at all, including my parents, and I really regretted the decision to agree to the magazine deal. By the time we'd finished all the photos, everyone was drunk – apart from us. So far, I'd had about half a glass of champagne and I was desperate for a full one or, better still, a bottle!

Once we joined the reception, though, and finally got a drink, the rest of the day passed in one big happy blur. It was only when Pete and I got to our hotel room, around 3am, and he turned to me and said, 'Hello, Mrs Walton' and I said, 'Well, hello, Mr Walton,' that it sank in. I suddenly realised, God, I'm a Mrs – I must remember to change my passport! We held each other all night and eventually made love.

Our honeymoon accommodation was a beautiful villa in the mountains of Spanish Catalonia. We'd arrived at night and couldn't find it at first and when we finally did we couldn't get in, as we'd been given the wrong key. Eventually, we found our way in and were blown away. On the outside, the villa just looked like any other, but inside it was amazing, with stunning décor, and champagne, flowers and food had been laid on by Shanti and the magazine. Everything we could have wished for had been prepared for us; it was bliss – finally! I'd just about forgiven the magazine when, the next morning, their photographers woke us up to take more pictures! We did the shoot, then had a late lunch and eventually they left. Actually, they were lovely and it wasn't their fault – but I was married now and just wanted to be alone with my husband. And at last we were free to enjoy ourselves in peace. Even so, to avoid any attention, we stayed out of the main towns and found a special restaurant in Madremanya, which was to be 'our special place'. An old converted watermill with a big stone courtyard looking out over cornfields, it was beautiful and so romantic – perfect for newly-weds.

The two weeks flashed by harmoniously and on the last night we wanted to go back there but when we rang we were told the restaurant was fully booked. 'Bugger it,' Pete said, 'we'll go down anyway and blag it.' He could see I really wanted to eat there again and was determined to get us in.

An hour or so later, we arrived and I walked straight up to the maitre d' and asked for a table for two for Walton. 'I'm sorry,' he said, 'we don't have you down.' Pete told him that was impossible, as we'd booked three days earlier and tonight was the last night of our honeymoon. With a sympathetic look on his face, the maitre d' said, 'Let me see what I can do.' Because we were out in the sticks they didn't recognise us, but within minutes they'd organised a table right at the front of the courtyard, where there was a little bit of spare space. We ended up with probably the best view in the house and they even gave us the wine for free!

We had a wonderful meal and as the sun went down Pete looked across at me and told me he loved me and how much he was looking forward to spending his life with me. I smiled and told him I felt exactly the same. As we held hands, I looked into the sunset and thought back to the time I'd left Geldof in the Chase Hotel, vowing to make something of my life. Now, ten years later, here I was sitting opposite my new husband, absolutely in love with him, and in two days I would be back filming my role as Kim Tate in *Emmerdale* which had made me one of the UK's most popular soap actresses.

Yes, I said to myself, you've done it! Life is perfect.

# 18

# Hollywood Calling

Things never stay rosy for long, do they?

Pete and I were to attend more than one funeral over the coming months. My Grandpa Leslie had been ill for some time and after we visited him in hospital I knew that would be the last time I'd see him – and it was. A true gentleman, he was sorely missed. Not long after, Grandma Kathleen died while Pete and I were visiting his parents in New Zealand, so in a few short months I'd lost both my remaining grandparents, which made me very sad.

On top of this, I'd recently been feeling less than my usual self. I'd always had bad aches and pains in my knees, which I'd assumed was just general wear and tear from riding, but when the pain spread to the joints in my hands and feet I thought a check-up was in order. Eventually, after I'd undergone various tests and been referred to hospital for X-rays, I was diagnosed with rheumatoid arthritis. I was devastated. I'd always imagined this illness affected only old people, but the doctor told me that it could strike people of all ages and, unluckily for me, I'd been struck at 31.

I felt really awful and was put on various tablets – which I took religiously – but nothing seemed to work. Dad had retired by now, and Piers had continued the business, changing its name to Hellenia and expanding it to incorporate natural health supplements. When I mentioned my diagnosis to him, he suggested I try MSM capsules, a new supplement the company was making. I'd not heard of MSM and Piers explained that it was a natural sulphur-based product known for its anti-inflammatory properties. Desperate for anything to relieve the symptoms, I started taking the capsules, and it wasn't long before I found myself apologising to my mum for previously dismissing herbal remedies as rubbish, because after a few weeks I suddenly started to feel much better.

Now I had that problem under control, Pete and I got on with trying to sell our cottages; both had been on the market for ages with no buyers forthcoming. We were finding the delay really frustrating because we'd recently viewed our dream home – a converted barn several miles out of Harrogate with stunning views over the Nidderdale valley. The moment we saw it we knew it was the one for us. At 232K, it was above Pete's comfort level, but not mine, and after lengthy discussions I won. Risking our finances, we managed to buy it and move in while still waiting for the cottages to sell.

I reasoned with Pete that now we had a house with a lot of land we could definitely get a dog. He'd always said we didn't have the space, but there was no excuse now. Within a month of moving in and, by chance, on our first wedding anniversary, 'our baby' arrived – a beautiful black Labrador puppy. We named him Digger, and our family was complete!

I was never one of those women who dream of having a baby – dogs and horses, yes, but babies, no – so our decision not to have children was one I accepted easily. Pete seemed happy enough for us to just have Thomas from time to time, and I'd grown to love him as my own, so there didn't seem any need to add to our 'family'. He also reminded me that not having children together would give us the freedom to do as we pleased, and since we both loved to travel it seemed like the right choice for us. Besides, I had four costly charges already – my racehorses.

My work was busier than ever, as I was in the middle of filming the exit of Ian Kelsey (who played my lover, Dave Glover) from the show. Ian had said he wanted to leave earlier that year, so the producers gave us 'the great fire storyline', where he would die saving our baby son, James. It was a bit of a palaver because the scenes weren't filmed in story order. First, we shot the hospital scenes, where Dave dies and I'm by his bedside, and to make us look like we'd been in the fire, the make-up team had smeared our faces with a black powder. Yet, when we filmed the fire scenes a week later, we were given barely any darkening make-up, so when the scenes were cut together the colour of our faces didn't match the story. This didn't seem to matter to the viewers, though, as the storyline was a massive success. It was certainly one of my all-time favourites.

But even though I knew I was in one of the top-rated shows on television and my character was probably one of the very best around, I couldn't shake the feeling that I was getting what my mum would call 'itchy feet' – and so was Pete.

We'd both been in the show since 1989 and it was now 1995, and I'd just started to feel that there must be more to working than playing one person. I wanted to move on. We also lost a few great mates that year, including Moley, who was a real character. He used to drive to *Emmerdale* in his tank – a real one. It did just five miles an hour and cost £200 in fuel for the journey, but he still drove it into work – in full camouflage! He certainly wasn't run-of-the-mill and you just had to accept him as he was. And we lost Peter Wren, a stage manager, who looked like the fourth member of the Bee Gees and drank Campari and soda by the bucket! He was a lovely man too and they were both close friends of ours, so it was doubly sad to lose them so close together.

Peter did the eulogy and gave Moley and Peter a great send-off, but it all heightened the feeling we shared that maybe an end of an era was coming. And a few days later even more devastating news followed. Pete received a call from his father, Brian, to say his mum had passed away. Mollie had been battling cancer for the past ten years but it was still a huge shock for us both, and Pete was devastated. At *Emmerdale*, they were really good about it and immediately wrote him out for two weeks, as well as booking his flights so he could attend the funeral. Unfortunately, they couldn't spare me, so I had to stay behind, which was gutting, as I really wanted to be there for him.

A few months earlier, the show's makers, Yorkshire Television, had announced that, because we were now more popular than ever, we would be extended from three times a week to four, having already gone from two to three the year before. It was great that we were doing so well, but, because the Tates were such a major family in the show, most of the storylines seemed to involve Peter and me, and as my workload increased hugely I just couldn't seem to shake off the tiredness that kept washing over me.

People outside the show had been telling me to leave before I became pigeon-holed, but it's difficult to make that leap once you've become settled and the money is good. Besides, it's always scary to leave such a big show, because you think you might not work again. I was well aware that this had happened to several *Emmerdale* cast members. Also, I knew I'd miss all my friends if I did go and, although I was often tired, Richard Thorp (who played Alan Turner), Johnny Leeze (Ned Glover), Ian Kelsey (before he left), Paul Lochran (Butch Dingle) and Roberta Carr (Jan Glover) were always on for a boozy lunch to keep your spirits up. Roberta was a dreadful corpser, so whenever I filmed with her we'd always had a laugh – even when it wasn't intentional!

Because I was now an established member of the cast, the writers looked after me very well, continually giving me great storylines. This was fantastic, but you didn't get any input in the show – it was always down to the writers and even when they came to the pub we weren't allowed to speak to them about ideas – so it started to become frustrating. After talking about the frustrations we felt at work, Pete and I arranged a meeting with our joint agent, David Daly, to tell him we were both thinking of leaving the show. On hearing this news, David went quiet for a moment and then said that it was probably best if Peter left first, as he had a greater chance of getting other work than I did. This really stung because, although Peter had been established in the business longer than me, I was one of the most successful soap actresses around at the time. I couldn't imagine Michelle Collins, who had just left *EastEnders* and seemed to have several shows on the go, had been told this by *her* agent.

Not wanting to cause a fuss, I nodded at what was being said and listened as David repeated the old clichés about how there are always more roles for men and what a tough industry it is for women. Sadly, I would go on to find out that such clichés were true, but it wasn't the best time to have heard them.

By now, I was quite confused, but I thought to myself, It's my decision, so I'll do what I think is best – when *I* think the time is right. I didn't say anything, though, as I'd decided to mull it over, but, as my new contract was about to be signed, I knew I couldn't wait long if I wanted to make a break.

The next day, I woke up and just knew I was going to tell the show's bosses that I wanted to leave – today. Inside, I felt that now was the right time to go. I was feeling I had nothing left to give, but, looking back, I know now I was just exhausted. I was also thinking that, with the show at an all-time high, if I stayed too long no one would ever think of me as anything other than Kim Tate and I really did want to see what else I could do.

So, after telling Pete, who said I had to do what 'felt right', I drove into the studio early and went straight to see the executive producer, Keith Richardson. Once I'd sat down with him, I came straight out with it. 'I'm not sure I want to renew my contact,' I told him. 'Actually, forget that – I know I *don't* want to renew my contract and I'd like to leave in '96.'

Keith looked really shocked and tried to talk me out of it, but I still said no. He knew me well enough to know that once I'd made up my mind there was no stopping me. Once they realised I couldn't be persuaded, they were very kind and said, 'Well, we're really sorry to see you go, but, if you're sure, then we'll give you a great exit.'

When the news got out, people were really shocked, as everyone had thought Pete would be the first to go. No one on set could believe I was ready to leave television's favourite 'bad girl' behind, but I felt I'd done everything I could with Kim at this point and I didn't want the fans to get bored with her, so I stuck to my decision in spite of the reactions. When it became known that I was to be dispatched in the 'Frank kills Kim in the quarry' storyline, Norman's mood on set was more than happy. Little did he know that things weren't quite as final as he might have hoped.

I filmed my exit storyline utterly exhausted. After Kim fakes her death in the hope that Frank will be blamed for her murder, he is charged and held in jail on remand. On my last day of filming, I was told I'd have to retake the final scene as it hadn't come out as they'd wanted. This surprised me because I knew it was as close to perfect as we could have got it, and I was a bit annoyed, as I just wanted to go home to bed.

We started again and halfway through the retake Pete appeared with a massive tray of champagne for the cast and crew and announced that everyone would miss me – especially him. I was fine until then, but when everyone raised their glass to toast me I burst into tears. It was the end of a chapter in my life, and I realised that I would miss them all and hoped I'd made the right decision.

I finally left the show after a tearful – yes, another – goodbye party, hosted by Johnny Leeze, Paul Fox, who played Will Cairns (and would later play Mike Baldwin's son Mark in *Coronation Street*), and me – it was a mass exodus! And a great do, to which my parents came and even brought Digger. When I eventually got home, I went straight to bed and hardly got up for a week. I was fully rested and starting to really enjoy having some time for myself, when the home phone rang and I answered a call that was about to make me do a complete U-turn.

'Hello,' I said, looking at myself in the mirror by the phone and thinking how much better I looked for having had a break.

'Hi, Claire,' Keith Richardson's deep Scottish voice rang out. 'We've got a brilliant storyline ready to bring you back if you fancy it.'

'But Kim's dead!' I said, not sure if he was having me on.

'No, she isn't,' he replied in a tone that made it clear he definitely wasn't joking.

Intrigued, I paused for a moment. 'Tell me more,' I said, and listened to his plan to bring back Kim. Frank would be released from remand in time to coincide with Kim's sudden reappearance, he explained. She would turn up at Home Farm when he was alone at night and the shock of seeing her 'back from the dead' would cause Frank, whose heart had weakened in prison, to suffer a fatal heart attack. Kim would then stand by laughing at her husband as he clutched his chest and pleaded for the tablets that could save his life. She would taunt him by waving them in front of him until he died, ultimately feeling that she'd gained revenge for her lover Dave's death, for which she blamed him.

With Frank gone, she would inherit the Tate empire, which he had built up from nothing, and would go on to wield the power that she had grown to love, before finding new love with Steve Marchant, and marrying him then eventually leaving again. Phew! Can you see now, dear reader, why I was always knackered?

Well, what actress could turn down storylines like that? Not this one, for sure! Although I knew immediately that Kim and I just had to do it, I told Keith I'd give it some serious thought and get back to him as soon as I knew what I wanted to do. I've never been one to make a decision on the spot. I know I'd been looking forward to taking time out for my horses and my home life and to get my teeth into a new role, but the invitation seemed too tempting to dismiss.

When Pete came home, I told him what had happened and he said that, if I did want to go back, now was the perfect time to make sure that there would be extra benefits for me when I returned. It was clear they were desperate to get me back, so now was the time to barter. After speaking to my agent, I decided that I did quite fancy another crack at Kim. It sounds odd, I know, after I'd gone to all that effort to leave, and requesting that Kim be killed off – so that going back was not an option – but the storyline just seemed right for her and the audience had never been entirely comfortable with the thought that she'd had to die – as they believed.

It was *Emmerdale*'s Christmas break, so Pete and I took off to do some travelling around South Africa, taking in Victoria Falls in Zimbabwe, Botswana and Namibia, where I visited the Africat cheetah charity, of which I was a patron. We then went on to Mauritius to finish our trip with a week on the beach. Well, that was the idea but we weren't very impressed with the island, and headed home early. We'd intended to do quite a bit of diving but found it severely over-dived, with nothing much left to see.

A couple of weeks later, I went to see Keith and laid down my three conditions. 1: as I'd only just left the show, a few months off before starting again; 2: I wanted a pay rise; and finally, two new projects to be reserved for me for after my new contract finished (I originally agreed to return for just eight months but ended up staying closer to 18). Keith seemed agreeable but I repeated my third condition, as I knew I was taking a risk returning when I should really have been broadening my CV. 'I'll come back in five months if you *absolutely* promise that I'll *definitely* have those two projects waiting for me at the end of my stint,' I told him and the production team. Everyone agreed and the deal was done.

Five months later, I returned to the set and everyone seemed genuinely pleased to see me. Well, almost everyone.

Poor Norman, who'd probably thought, Great, I've seen her off. Now here I was back from the dead and about to kill him! It must have been a massive shock when he was told, but, to be fair to him, he was very professional about it. It would have pissed me off if I'd been in his position.

As I got stuck into my new scenes, I suddenly rediscovered the same passion for Kim's character that I'd felt in the beginning. Obviously, I'd just badly needed a break. I was now feeling more than up for the challenges that lay ahead, which was just as well, as over the next few months Kim featured in nearly all the show's major storylines. The scene where she kills Frank turned out to be one of the most celebrated scenes in soap history. The writing was superb and Kim reached new heights of evil when, with Frank begging for the heart pills that she has in her hands that could save his life, she just watches him, smirking until he expires at her feet. Norman took ages to 'die' and we were all keen to see his fingers finally stop twitching so we could finish the scene! When I later remarked that it would have been quicker if I'd been allowed to bash his head in, this must have created a vision they liked the sound of, as that was what Kim would do to Pete's Chris Tate before I left for the final time.

When Frank dies, Kim leans over him and uses her compact mirror to first check he is actually dead and then to reapply her make-up! Pure camp classic bitch behaviour and a scene that continues to see Kim Tate often feature in those 'top ten television bitches of all time' programmes that come out every so often. Kim then becomes lady of the manor and over the next few months rolls around fighting Zoe on Frank's grave, throws people down stairs, sacks all the members of the village who work for her (apart from her beloved Seth!) and, once she has accomplished all these, plots revenge on the Tate family.

When Steve Marchant, played by Paul Opacic, comes into her life they pull off a stolen stallion scam that eventually leads to another wedding and Kim escaping in a helicopter with half a million in cash after tipping Chris out of his wheelchair and hitting him over the head with a bowling ball.

It was knackering. Pete and I were in the studio for three

days solid and filmed 75 scenes one after the other – a record for *Emmerdale*. We thought we'd been tired before, but now we really knew what the word meant.

Two days before I was due to film my last-ever scenes of *Emmerdale*, my agent called saying that he'd been approached about the possibility of my playing the co-lead opposite the Hollywood actress Rosanna Arquette, whom I'd loved in *Desperately Seeking Susan*. The film was *Interview with a Dead Man* and was being funded by Canada and Spain and shot on the Isle of Man because of its tax concessions. Someone had dropped out of the role of the 'bad sister' and my name had been suggested by the director, Stuart St Paul, who'd previously worked with me on *Emmerdale*. The film bosses were interested but said they needed to know how big a name I was, so I had to put together my entire collection of front covers and press cuttings.

After they'd seen the pack, David called to say they wanted me and I'd have to be on location in three days. I was now on my last day of *Emmerdale*, and I thought, God, I've got a Hollywood movie on my day of leaving – fantastic! I couldn't wait to get out of there and as soon as we wrapped I rushed off home to pack. The day after, as Pete kissed me goodbye at the airport, he was nearly as excited for me as I was.

When I arrived at our location, Simon Callow and some other members of the cast were filming elsewhere on the island. Simon had just had a big hit with *Four Weddings and a Funeral* and turned out to be just as funny off-screen as on. Meanwhile, I asked the crew what Rosanna was like and I was told they'd never met her, as she hadn't arrived on set yet. The director assured me that it was common practice to shoot so as to fit in with Hollywood stars, so I thought nothing more of it and continued filming my scenes until the Christmas break. I assumed this would be the customary few days but, when I was told it was two weeks, Pete and I decided to fly to Grenada with my parents. I couldn't believe how much more flexible shooting movies was compared with TV work and we had a wonderful holiday, spending most of the time on the beach drinking cocktails, with me learning my lines.

Back home after our break, I was surprised to find no call time had been left on my answering machine, as I was due on set the next day. When I called the third assistant director, he said he was surprised I hadn't heard from my agent, because the film's finance had been pulled and the movie was off. I was out on my ear, as were the rest of the cast, and none of us was likely to be paid; well, no one apart from Rosanna, who allegedly received $1 million. I was devastated and can see now that this is why I retreated back to television. Everyone had told me to go and try Hollywood, but, if this was Hollywood, I was staying put.

I've since realised that this happens a lot in the independent film world, but it wouldn't have been much consolation at the time. Before going in search of the next job, I decided to have a rest and recover from Kim's exit storyline, which was currently going out to rave reviews on ITV. I don't mind having some time off, I thought, after

s Karen Betts in *Bad Girls*, pictured with Jim Fenner, who was played by Jack Ellis.

*Above*: One of many on-screen altercations with the nasty prison officer Fenner.

*Below*: Incarcerated for a publicity shot with the other cast members of the show!

Heaven! Pete and I on holiday in Bora Bora in the South Pacific.

*Inset*: Undoubtedly the way to dine!

Happier times for Pete and I than were to come.

*Above*: In Auckland, visiting Pete's parents.

*Below*: A merry Christmas with the family at Roseberry Cottage. *From left to right*: Dad, Aunty Elaine, Uncle Peter, Piers, Cousin Anna, me and Pete.

*above*: With Fergal Lynch, Kieren Fallon and Sean Lynch at the Breeders Cup in Santa Anita, 2003.

*below left*: Me and 'my boys', celebrating at Gary Stevens' house after Kieren won in the fillies and mares turf race. *From left to right*: Gary, Sean, and Kieren.

*below right*: With David Craig at the Ripley Horse Show.

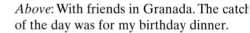

*Above*: With friends in Granada. The catch of the day was for my birthday dinner.

*Below*: The opening of John Carroll's pub, The Manor Inn, at Cockerham. From left right: Craig Wilkinson, John, George Duffield, Frankie Dettori, me, Jack Berry and Dietmar Harmann.

*Inset*: Real-life bad girls! In Alcatraz with Clare Pears and Fiona Mallidi (née McKie

*above*: My beautiful horse, King's Rock, being ridden to victory by Neil Callan at Leicester in 2004.

*below left*: At home with Boomshadow.

*below right*: Digger, my favourite boy.

I've had a tough time over the last few years but I'm now feeling better than ever, and a
ready for the next amazing chapter of my life ...

three weeks had gone by and my agent still hadn't called with anything majorly exciting. Don't panic – you've still got those two projects at Granada waiting (Granada had taken over Yorkshire Television before I left), I reminded myself and set about enjoying the rare free time I had by seeing old friends and racing my horses.

Les Eyre claimed a horse for my syndicate called Moonlight Flit, and she was entered in a race at Southwell on 22 March 1999. An owner can enter their horse in a claiming race for an amount that they are prepared to sell him for, should a buyer put in a 'claim'. Horses are not always claimed, but that's a risk you have to take. My friend David Craig drove me there and on the way we had several phone calls all predicting that Moonlight Flit was going to win, and she did – my first winner as an owner. I felt like I'd won the Derby! Les had also got me involved in a new partnership with the Hyde family, Judith, Jeff (who is no longer with us, sadly) and their son David. We had bought a big chestnut colt and called him Pentagon Lad and, six weeks after Moonlight's win, he won a race at Carlisle – the first of many for him.

Around this time, Pete was approached by ITV with an invitation for me to appear on *This Is Your Life*. We'd always joked that if either of us was asked we'd say no, as we found it embarrassing not knowing who would turn up from your past – or present! So I turned it down. But, when I was asked to do ITV's *Star Lives* with Carol Vorderman, I agreed because I had control over the guests, and it was quite well paid. Because Ms Vorderman couldn't travel to Leeds, they flew all my friends and family to the studio, including my poor dad – who had to fly separately as the first plane couldn't accommodate his wheelchair – and Clare and Fiona, who were flown in from abroad. Les Eyre even left his native Yorkshire to appear, which was a rarity for him, so I was touched.

Some weeks later, I was just about to go for a ride when the phone rang. Dashing back inside and nearly falling over Digger, who thought I was playing a chase-me game, I answered.

'You've been nominated for the best exit at the Soap Awards,' my agent said.

Pleased as I was at the nomination, I felt a bit disappointed that this was all that was on offer. 'OK, great. I'll go,' I told him. 'But, David, can you call Granada and see what's happening with those projects I'm supposed to be choosing from?'

Little did I know that I would soon find out that the deal to offer me two projects would prove ineffective – or that attending the Soap Awards would end up landing me in prison.

I went along just wanting to have a good time at the awards, not giving mine much thought, and after we'd all got stuck into the free bar I made my way into the auditorium for the announcements. The awards weren't televised then, so it was quite informal. I was sitting between Leah and Pete and we were chatting quietly as the nominations were announced. I couldn't believe it when I heard my name: Kim's departure from the show had been judged Best Exit! Surprised, I made my way to the podium and thanked everyone, making it clear that I was picking up the award as much for the writers as for myself, since Kim's bumpy road throughout my *Emmerdale* days was down to them. I did, however, make one big boo-boo – I thanked everyone I'd ever worked with, the world and his wife, but actually forgot to thank the one person I filmed all my exit scenes with – Peter! I think he's since forgiven me. It was lovely to win, albeit in a strange category.

We'd been at the bash for a couple more hours and I was starting to make my way out when an attractive man in his mid-thirties came over and introduced himself as Brian Park of Shed Productions. I knew instantly who he was, as he was well known in TV land as the 'Axe Man' for his brief stint on *Coronation Street*, where he provoked outrage by killing off *Street* favourite Derek Wilton with a heart attack under a giant paperclip! He asked me if I wanted to have a drink with him as he had a project he wanted to tell me about. I'd already heard he had a new show starting called *Bad Girls*, a female prison drama that I thought sounded interesting, and here was my chance to pick the man's brains! We sat down and chatted about what I'd been doing, Brian saying he was a huge fan of Kim Tate and that he might have something for me in *Bad Girls*, but he wasn't sure yet.

'Well, I'm up for anything, so feel free to give my agent a shout if you want to see me,' I said. After that, we shared some laughs and when I left Brian said he'd keep me in mind.

Some months passed and I'd been up for a few roles and

started jobbing around. I did an episode of the ill-fated ITV show *Babes in the Wood* with Denise Van Outen – the worst job I've ever done! – and I guest-starred in BBC's *Doctors*, but nothing I could really get my teeth into.

I'd just returned from Las Vegas from Clare Pears's wedding to Paul O'Brien, and Pete and Digger and I were snuggled up in front of the TV as I switched channels to the opening credits of *Bad Girls*. 'This is what Brian Park's company makes,' I said to Pete and we settled down to watch the show. It was gripping, dramatic, pretty close to the bone and controversial. I was hooked! It was like nothing else that was on at the time. 'I'd love to be in this,' I said to Pete, who agreed that it was quite good. I flicked on the kettle, wondering if Brian Park would call or if it had been just 'TV talk'.

# 19

# Behind Bars

Yes! I thought. My agent had just rung with the news that Brian Park had finally phoned the office to say he'd like to see me about going on Bad Girls. It had been six weeks since that night at the Soap Awards and I was more than ready to get back to work full-time.

Pete and I had watched the first few episodes of *Bad Girls* and we were now really into it, as those first few episodes had everything: lesbian inmates, bent screws and dangerous women. It was just what I'd been looking for; I loved it and I wanted in! It was an instant hit with many other viewers too, especially the lesbian community, who, as the Nikki and Helen love story slowly unfolded, raising many an eyebrow (and the temperature) in living rooms across the country, took the series to their hearts (and naughty minds, if the fan mail I would receive later was anything to go by). I liked the fact that the show wasn't too soapy and raised issues about an inept justice system and inmates' bad treatment at the hands of prison officers. Gritty, strong and totally compelling, it was certainly a rival to *The Governor* or *Within These Walls*, which I'd loved – good old Googie Withers!

David said Brian had invited me to meet him at his home and in this business that is a very good sign – unless your host is planning to pounce on you! But, knowing Brian was of a different persuasion, I was pretty sure I was off to talk business with him. So, the following Tuesday, I took a train from York down to London, then jumped in a cab for the short ride to his house in Islington. When he opened the big black door of the Victorian terrace, he greeted me with: 'Do you want tea, coffee or red wine?'

'Oh, red wine, please!' I said.

He smiled and lead me down to the kitchen, where we quickly polished off a couple of bottles of wine while chatting about the show. I told Brian my impressions of it and he explained what he felt I could bring to the second series. With the basics out of the way, we opened another bottle and Brian, amused that I was holding up my glass to be filled again and looking not at all drunk – thank God I can hold my booze! – said, 'Now I know you can drink, the job's yours!' I was thrilled and we toasted the second series before I staggered off to catch the train home, merry in both senses of the word.

When the details came through, I learned that I would be going into the show as a prison officer called Karen Betts, who would soon go on to become the new wing governor, a role at that time being played by Simone Lahbib. When I read the character and storyline breakdowns, I realised Karen was about as different from Kim as she could be. Where Kim might well have ended up behind the bars of a women's prison, Karen was definitely a rule-enforcer rather than a rule-breaker. Once installed as wing governor, she was a stickler for the rules and never suffered fools gladly; she was quite straight-laced and her 'genuine goodness' regularly brought her into direct conflict with inmates and officers alike. From reading quite a few of her scripts, I could see that she seemed very level-headed, efficient and pragmatic, never allowing her emotions to rule her head.

I was just beginning to think there was no wild side at all to Karen Betts when it was revealed that she had a weakness for 'bastards' and would soon be in a very volatile relationship with the show's resident baddie, Jim Fenner, excellently played by Jack Ellis. They had dated before and he would eventually rape her and set her up for murder. Nice! I thought. Something to get my teeth into.

Unbeknown to me at the time, my casting had followed some 'politics' within the show. The ITV Network apparently wanted to re-jig the role of the current governor, Helen Stewart. At their request, I'd been drafted in to work with a changed storyline in which Helen resigns as wing governor and Karen takes over. When I started on the show, I was completely unaware of this. I wouldn't know until later that essentially I'd been brought in to take someone else's job and when I found out I felt really bad.

But it wasn't my fault and, because the decision had come from 'up above', Brian had had to do it that way. There was never any slight on Simone as an actress – they'd just wanted a different direction for the wing governor – so he was able to quickly bring her character back in a different role. Brian was always loyal as a producer and, when Simone returned, the network seemed more than happy and she went on to become even more popular in Helen Stewart's new role as the prison's liaison officer. Helen and Nikki, played by Mandana Jones, became the audience's firm favourites as a result of their tortured love affair – so all's well that ends well. Thank God I hadn't known on my first day what had been going on, as I was nervous enough as it was.

I started shooting my scenes on the Larkhall Prison set at Three Mills Studios in Bow, in the East End, in July 1999 and we finished the following March. After my nine years on *Emmerdale*, where we'd all got to know one another so well, it was weird to be on such a big set among strangers. As the new girl, at first I found it nerve-racking. Am I going to fuck this up? I kept thinking. Am I a blagger? I was still unsure of my abilities and kept telling myself I was getting away with it rather than that I deserved to be there. It's funny really, because friends of mine have said that I should have been over- rather than under-confident after all my success with Kim, but that's just me. My first scenes were with Helen Fraser, who played Body Bag, and Jack Ellis and, as it turned out, everyone was really nice and after a few days I felt I fitted in OK.

When the second series aired, the reviews were good but I was a bit surprised that the amount of press I was being offered wasn't huge. I was still getting lots of attention courtesy of Kim but, because *Bad Girls* was more of an ensemble piece, when I was asked to do press it was often with others. In fact, although it led to my profile dipping somewhat, this worked out quite well at the time, as it's a relief to not have to think of something new to say to a journalist every day.

As shooting of the third series rumbled on, I began to feel that Karen's role in the show seemed to be mainly passing blocks of information to the audience and not really getting the juicy storylines for herself. The first two series had been pretty hard hitting and dealt with controversial issues that would affect women in a real prison, whereas the third series seemed to move away from serious issues and to gravitate towards outrageous storylines, bringing a much camper tone to the show.

Over the next year or so, I seemed to drive endlessly up and down the A1 between North Yorkshire and London. Nowadays, whenever I went home, Peter just didn't seem himself. He would stay up late watching TV while I waited for him in bed and, although we'd always had quite an active sex life, now we were barely having sex at all. At the time, I put it down to stress and the fact that he was desperate to leave *Emmerdale*.

Chris Tate was still one of the show's most popular characters and Pete's schedule was even more gruelling (as mine had become as Kim responded to ever more public demand) because it had now gone to five episodes a week. So I could understand if he was run down and not in the best of moods. I decided that, if I did two more series of *Bad Girls* and Peter left *Emmerdale* around the time he hoped to, in 18 months, we could perhaps start spending quality time together, because it was the lack of this, I felt, that had caused us to drift apart. I was sure we were just going through a difficult patch, like most married people do, and I certainly didn't think it was serious. In any case, Pete wasn't the only thing on my mind when a string of equine catastrophes came my way.

The news that my horse Pentagon Lad had died from an undiagnosed intestinal disease came as a devastating blow, as his career was in full flow and he'd won over £50,000 in prize money, more than paying his way. Les Eyre, who was about to retire to Spain, which also saddened me, as he was a great mate, suggested we buy Pentagon Lad's full sister. This we did, but unfortunately Pentagon Lady fell ill with the same condition and had to be put down. To take my mind off these losses, I put all my attention on to my new colt, of the Sri Pekan line, and tried to get my parents, who already had two unraced horses with Les, involved with him. But, after the deaths of Pentagon Lad and Lady, my partners in those horses, Jeff and Judith Hyde, decided they now wanted to come in on my new horse, which was a shame because it meant I couldn't bring my parents in. We eventually named him Creskeld, after Creskeld Hall, the house used as *Emmerdale*'s Home Farm, and Creskeld Lane, where the Hydes lived, so it seemed the perfect choice.

I then decided that I really wanted a horse just for myself, and Les and I agreed that I could take Boomshadow, a horse we'd previously syndicated without winning anything much, home to ride as a hack. I stabled him at my friend Tasha's, across the fields from my house, and really enjoyed the afternoons I spent with him. Unfortunately, because he had been hit by a truck as a youngster in an incident I hadn't been made aware of, he was terribly nervous of traffic, and before long I had to let him go to another home.

With my dad's mobility declining further, my parents were forced to sell our family home and have a new house built where he could conveniently use his wheelchair. It was sad to see the family house go, but it was clear to all that this was the right decision. The strain of looking after Dad on her own had started to show on my mum and they decided to take on a full-time carer to lighten the load. Gabi soon became like one of the family.

Back in London, I myself had started looking for a house to buy, as hotels are not just impersonal but also impossible to work from while filming at night. After looking at a few places, I found a lovely brand-new duplex flat in a modern complex in Stoke Newington. I was pleased to have somewhere of my own to go to after a long shoot.

When the third series of *Bad Girls* went out, I was nominated a second time for Best Actress at the *TV Quick* Awards. I'd lost the year before, so I didn't hold out much hope, but that night, at the Dorchester Hotel, I won. It was so lovely to win it, because it was voted for by the audience and they are the ones who really matter. The winners were decided by telephone votes, so when I went up to collect my award I said, 'My mum must have been very busy voting. Now I know why her line was always engaged!', which brought the house down.

I would never go on the way some people do, thanking everyone from their manager to their hairdresser. No one really likes a diva – apart perhaps from gay men, though even they don't when they actually meet one – and I think because I never played the prima donna I managed to avoid any tension with the rest of the cast when I won awards. In fact, that's not quite accurate, as the following year I won Best Actress again and there was one comment that surprised me a little. This came from Debra Stephenson, who played Shell Dockley, during a conversation about soaps versus dramas. Debra said that she'd 'never do a soap', which immediately poured shit on nearly nine years of my career and something I was very proud of. I can't understand why people get snooty about soaps, but there are still people in the industry who have a blinkered attitude to the genre. But I must say I smiled to myself when I saw Debra had joined *Coronation Street* – one of the nation's biggest soaps and by far the longest-running. She must have changed her mind.

Later that night, I bumped into Vinnie Jones, whom I hadn't seen since our night together. He patted my bum at the bar and said, 'All right, gal? You've done all right for yourself.'

I laughed and told him, 'You've done pretty good too.'

*Lock, Stock* had been huge by then, and Vinnie knew it. We laughed and had a drink and chatted about what we'd been doing over the years, then I went home to take my heels off – I'd been on set all day and my feet were killing me.

In the studio car on my way home to Stoke Newington, my mind began to drift to Peter. I'd called him at home but there was no answer. Come to think of it, these days there was hardly ever an answer when I called. I knew he was mad-busy filming, just as I was, but no one is on that many night shoots, I thought. The niggling feeling that I'd had for some time sprang up again and I couldn't ignore it any longer. As I got out of the car and thanked my driver, Peter was still on my mind.

My award under my arm, I opened the front door, went inside, lit a cigarette, poured myself a glass of wine and finally considered the possibility that my marriage was drifting away from me. Even though I'd been working in London a lot, I'd been making every effort to travel home to Yorkshire every Friday when I'd finished shooting. We had also been shooting the exterior prison scenes on location in Oxfordshire, which couldn't be helped, but it was another commitment keeping me away from home and taking its toll on my marriage. Working like this, you're almost leading two different lives and are never together. People used to say that to me and I'd think, Oh, yeah, as if that's what happens! But it does. Once you are both leading full-on, separate lives with new people around you, it takes some damn hard effort to pull the relationship together, which is why, despite being knackered, I was still travelling home every weekend.

By now, Peter was not coming to see me in London. I had new friends on set and they would come round to my place, which was fairly near the studio. The weekend shoots became more and more frequent, so now I wasn't even able to get home every weekend – and that wasn't helping either. Pete kept saying he really wanted to leave *Emmerdale* – but he said that every year. Whenever we did speak on the phone, it was as if he was a different person. He was no longer keen on racing, which was something we'd frequently had in common, but had got more into football. When I came home, he was always out and seldom waited in for me. In the early days, he used to cook a meal for me – spaghetti carbonara was his speciality – after my long drive, but not any more.

Pete seemed to be enjoying living his own life and I felt I was now surplus to requirements. I tried to talk to him about it but he just said that everything was fine, and that was how we went on. I never believed it would stay like that. Once I'm back home permanently, I thought, we'll get close again and we'll be all right. I still loved him and I would not give up my marriage without a fight.

On set, I smiled to hide my heartache. We did manage to have quite a few laughs and, considering there were so many women in the cast, there was surprisingly very little bitching. Once a week, the main cast would nip to the local shops and stock up on booze and various foods and then hotfoot it back to our specially built green room. A large garden shed on hefty 20-foot stilts, this was hardly glamorous but we made the best of it and our weekly ritual provided relief from a gruelling schedule that could demand up to 14 hours a day. It was always nice to relax up there for ten minutes or so, but it was a good job that what we called the 'the ski lodge' was so high up, as it meant that the actresses who liked to smoke dope – not mentioning any names but they all know who they are – could enjoy their rest time undetected.

Late one afternoon, my friend Lois Ward, a supporting artiste on the show, and I went for one of our regular dinners. I'd finished for the day and had the following day off, so we decided to make a night of it. We were on our fourth bottle in the restaurant, when my phone rang; it was Debbie, the third assistant director, who explained that I was needed for a pick-up, a re-shoot of a scene we'd already done, early the next morning. Lois was highly amused at my sudden plight until her phone rang too and her agent delivered the same news – we both had to be at work for 7am.

'Damn!' I said, as I looked at the half-full bottle of champagne in front of us. 'Well, Lois, we've started, so we might as well finish!' And I promptly ordered another bottle, the two of us having drunkenly decided that, as there was no dialogue required, we'd continue our night as planned and deal with our hangovers in the morning. However, when my alarm went off at 5.45am – I'd been in bed 45 minutes – the decision to have partied on suddenly seemed a bad idea. I dragged my clothes on and staggered out to the car, where Terry, my Liverpudlian driver, was waiting.

'Fucking hell, Claire – you smell like a brewery!' he said, as he opened the door for me. I managed about two words the whole journey and wished I'd been more sensible, but knowing that I only had a quick scene to do and then the whole day off (which I'd now be spending in bed) I went into make-up and got ready for the scene.

On set, the director asked me to walk through the prison gates, which Lois was to open for me, and turn right. 'Right? I said. 'But we never turn right.' There was no right turn on this side of the set – it was a no-through road.

'Yes, just turn right,' he said.

But, through force of habit and severe alcohol consumption, I turned left three takes in a row – much to the crew's amusement. After the third time, Dan Taylor, the art director, and Mark McQuoid, the cameraman, resorted to using big luminous arrows to point out the direction for me to follow. How embarrassing! But it had been my day off, so I didn't feel guilty as I weaved my way back to wardrobe after finally getting it right.

Dan and I became good mates, as we both loved practical jokes and were often to be found setting up crew members with a remote-controlled fart machine. Tony Pitts would have been proud of us. Dan later went on to flat-sit for me in London when I stopped working on *Bad Girls*, an arrangement which eventually inspired the press to declare he was my toy boy. One they definitely got wrong.

Drinking was also quite a big part of the social scene on

*Bad Girls*, as Tracey Wilkinson, who played Di Barker, would find out. Brian Park and I would occasionally have lunch, as we'd got quite close by series three, and one day went to eat at J. Sheekey in Covent Garden, where we ended up knocking back seven bottles of champagne. Wilko, as we called Tracey, later bet me that she could beat that total when Brian next took her to lunch but failed so miserably and got into such a state by the fourth bottle that Brian had to call Terry the driver to come and collect her, as no taxi driver would allow her in his cab!

One thing that really annoyed me at the time was that, although the *Bad Girls* office team knew that my main home was the farthest away and that I travelled back at weekends, they never took account of it when planning the filming schedule. I always asked very nicely, 'If at all possible, could you please not make my scenes the last to be filmed on Friday evenings or the first scenes to be shot on Monday mornings?' I knew that scheduling is beyond an actor's control but some members of the cast did only two days a week and occasionally they could have been used on a Friday or a Monday. Yet, despite my pleas, they always scheduled it so that I had two days off in the middle of the week and never at either end. This used to upset me because it was stopping me getting home at times and I knew, by the fact that Peter and I were communicating less and less, that there was serious trouble brewing. In my experience, absence does not make boys' hearts grow fonder, and it was this constant separation that was killing my marriage – or so I thought.

One day, I told Helen Fraser how I felt about the schedule and she said she'd had the same problem and when she'd asked about it she'd been told that it was because they knew we would deliver – 'at least you'll get it in one go' was the joke. She lived in Suffolk, so she was nearly as annoyed as I was.

On top of worrying about my marriage, I was increasingly uneasy over the direction in which my character, Karen, was going – in my opinion, down. While at first, I'd admired her controlled strength, now I was getting bored with her lack of excitement and I kept hoping she would become a bit ballsier. There were inklings of what she could be like when a slight rebellious streak occasionally shone through, but I knew she would never be allowed to take anything to extremes. Everything that she did was so controlled that I was starting to get frustrated. I wanted character development and maybe to see her go off the rails at some point. Even her career appeared to be on a slippery slope and, after the introduction of one or two new characters, I didn't think she was going to be in a very good position at all.

I wondered if what had happened to Simone's character was happening to mine. I would have given it more thought but right now I had more important things on my mind than Karen Betts's obvious downfall.

# 20

# Desperate Housewife

At home alone on a rare day off, I was unaware that among the post I was flicking through was some information that would bring my whole world crashing down and change everything forever.

I'd been getting ready to meet my ex-*Emmerdale* publicist Shanti in Leeds – we hadn't seen each other for a very long time – when one particular letter caught my eye. As I pulled the paper out from the small envelope, I saw the first words of the handwritten note: 'Your husband is having an affair with my wife.' I gripped the table as I sat down with shock. My beloved Digger seemed to sense something was wrong and immediately came and sat at my feet. I stroked him as I forced myself to read the rest of the letter, which was from the husband of Samantha Giles, who played the barmaid Bernice Blackstock in *Emmerdale*.

Pulling no punches, the letter stated in no uncertain terms that Peter was screwing Samantha and that I should know what he was like because it was my fault too. Somehow, I couldn't believe what I was reading, even though I knew instantly it was true. Then I thought, Hang on, I'm a victim here too, so why is he trying to hurt me by sending me a letter that is far from sympathetic to my feelings? He was clearly a man who wanted me to feel as bad as he did, and he had gone to no effort to even word the letter nicely. Maybe he thought I was like Kim Tate and deserved harsh words – but I was the innocent one here. He hadn't even bothered to give me any contact details so that I could discuss it with him – he'd just put his name: Nick.

At that moment, what pissed me off most was how Nick felt he had the right to write to me in such a hurtful way, and that somehow took the focus off the fact that my husband had been cheating on me for some time. And to discover it was someone Pete worked with, who would know a lot of the people we knew, was the sting in the tail. Apart from the pain in my heart, I felt humiliated.

Who knows? I thought. How has it come to this? I was also shocked that, if he was going to cheat on me, he should have chosen her. I'd worked with her only briefly before I'd left the show, but she hadn't struck me as his type at all. She certainly wasn't my type of person and I was at a loss to think that I might lose my husband to her. I never really suspected Pete would cheat on me, even though we were going through a bad patch. The odd thought that he might be seeing someone else had popped into my head when we'd stopped having sex, but I put it to the back of my mind. I just didn't believe he would do that to me, to *us*, as he'd never been that sort of man. But I couldn't do that now – I had the *letter* to deal with, and a lunch date with an old friend that I couldn't get out of.

Stuffing the letter in my bag, I drove off in a daze to meet Shanti with questions racing through my mind. How many people knew? Were people laughing at me? Had they done it in our home? In our bed?

Over lunch, I was so numb but I tried to seem myself; I must have done a decent job, as Shanti didn't notice anything was wrong. I said not a word about the letter and, after dropping her home, I pulled in and rang Peter's mobile. The call went through to the answering machine, as usual. 'I think we need to talk,' I said to the message service.

By the time I got home, his car was in the drive and he was indoors waiting. I parked, opened the front door and walked into the living room that had seen so many happy times. Normally I would shout 'hello' or something silly to let him know I was home, but this time I was silent. When I entered the kitchen, Peter was sitting on 'his' sofa in tears. He looked up at me and said he was sorry. It was clear he knew that I knew – *she* had told him that Nick had written to me – and he was crying really hard.

Instead of the anger I should have felt, I felt a surge of love when I looked at him. He must still care, I thought, otherwise he wouldn't be crying. I poured myself a

Jameson's and sat opposite him on 'my' sofa. My stomach was churning with such raw emotion that I felt I was going to be sick. I sipped my drink in a state of disbelief. Peter looked at me oddly, as I appeared to be quite calm. But I wasn't – it was just that my feelings seemed to have frozen and I couldn't take in what was happening; I felt almost as if I was in a trance. I wanted to ask him, Is this a joke? Of all the people it could have been – for it to be *her*. I just couldn't understand it; I would never have picked her for him in a million years. I watched him crying and wondered if I knew him at all.

Pete spoke first. 'I'm so, so sorry, I didn't mean to do it... Things were wrong with us – you were away. It's just something that happened... We were leading different lives...' All the old clichés came out of his mouth, yet when I looked at him and listened to him I could still see and hear my husband – the man I loved. I started crying too and we hugged and cried together.

The first words I found myself uttering were: 'So what are we going to do about it?'

He looked at me in shock – as if he believed that I wouldn't want him back – but this was my marriage and I wasn't going to give it up without a fight.

We stayed up all night talking about what had gone wrong. He blamed 'distance' and said he hadn't meant to start an affair but it was over now and he wanted to save our marriage. We slept in separate beds that night. I had the week off from *Bad Girls*, which was bloody lucky, as I don't think I could have dealt with working.

The next morning, I lay in bed wondering what to do. He'd hurt me, but I loved him. He'd said he was sorry, and no one is perfect, so surely our marriage was worth trying to resuscitate. He'd said it was over with her, so I decided to test him. I could hear his mobile ringing and him on the phone to her. I went downstairs and he followed me from one of the spare rooms and we sat in the kitchen. I made the tea and sat next to him. Digger was on the floor looking worried – he'd never seen his mum and dad like this and was uncharacteristically quiet. I knew I wasn't ready to give up on Pete yet.

'Look, you've been wrong,' I said, putting my hand on his. 'But I still love you. Do you want to fix this or...?

'Yes,' he interrupted, 'I do.'

So that was the start of our attempt to repair our nine-year marriage.

How sad it was that we had come to this, but I wasn't ready to throw in the towel just yet. We agreed that he'd tell her it was over for good when he met her later that day. She'd asked him to go and see her, as she was being followed by the press and was 'finding it hard to cope'. She couldn't handle the mayhem she'd helped to create and, because I was clearly stronger than her, I agreed to let him go.

When he returned, I told him I would forgive him and he promised he would make more of an effort to spend time with me. I felt I was just as guilty, because I hadn't been at home much and because I should have done something sooner, instead of letting it drift by and thinking

I could fix it later. Even though she was a complete bitch to start a full-on affair with my husband, having only recently married herself, it had taken four people to derail my marriage but hopefully the two important ones would be able to fix it. Samantha left *Emmerdale* shortly afterwards, which I was pleased about. I never heard from her at all.

It felt strange to think that only a year earlier I'd felt I had everything I'd ever wanted: a great career, a lovely home, no money worries and a wonderful marriage. But I now know nothing in the world is ever perfect and a good relationship needs work and that was why ours had started to fall apart. If anyone reading this can feel your partner drifting away, please don't ignore it; you have to stop and hit it head on.

And we didn't. So I can't blame Peter totally and can't blame her totally, but I won't blame myself totally either. As far as their affair goes, well, I understand feelings can't always be helped, but I believe full-on affairs sometimes can be. I tried to take everything on board that had happened but, despite knowing we were going to give our marriage another go, I just couldn't shake off the anger, the humiliation and the general depressed feeling of having been let down.

It was at this point that a mix of paranoia and embarrassment kicked in. My mind was racing with questions like: When did this start? Has he talked about me to her? Most of the *Emmerdale* cast must have known, as I knew how gossipy people can be on set, and suddenly it all started to make sense. I'd wondered why some of the cast at a recent awards ceremony had been looking over at me oddly and I remembered that Sheree Murphy, who played Tricia Dingle, appeared to be talking with Adele Silva and giving me funny looks. Now I knew why.

Mark Charnock and Jeff Hordley (who played Marlon and Cain Dingle) had come over when the girls were chatting and made a point of being really friendly towards me. They must have known and felt bad about it. It was very sweet but I couldn't help but feel angry that they'd even had to feel sorry for me. Just how many people bloody know? I thought.

'Has she been in my house – in our bed?' I asked Pete later. He said she hadn't, so I had to take his word for it. But I later found out that on a couple of occasions friends of Pete and I had been at my house when Samantha had just walked in, assuming he was alone. One pal walked out in protest but felt they couldn't tell me – which I understand now.

And now, as I prepared to return to London to shoot *Bad Girls*, the anger was really mounting. That's my house. How dare she come in and out of my home? Once those troubling thoughts came into my mind, I started to lose my cool. I'd been so calm before but now, as I realised how much had gone on behind my back, I saw that what was probably my best shot at a 'perfect marriage' and our life together had just been snatched away. The sacred trust had been broken; the vital element of respect damaged.

The last thing I wanted to do right now was work, but I had a job to do, and my problems were just that – mine.

# 21

# Love Me or Leave Me

Finally ariving home from London, I found several messages from Dad saying he'd been trying to reach me urgently. Oh, God, what's wrong? I thought. Praying it wasn't Mum or Pete, I called his number and waited for him to answer.

'Claire, I've been trying to get hold of you all night – your mobile was off.'

'What is it?' I said, as I sat on the sofa, worrying what was coming next.

'It's about Sarah Lunn – it's bad news.'

I immediately felt a massive rush of concern, as Sarah was a good friend. What on earth was he about to say? He went on to tell me that she'd been in a car crash the day before and had been killed instantly. I burst into tears and Pete, who had come into the living room during the call and heard what I'd said as I repeated the words in an effort to take them in, came over and put his arms around me. I spent an hour crying with Pete and talking about Sarah. She was so full of life and just 32. It seemed so unreal that she'd gone.

To try to take my mind off what Dad had told me, I started opening the post. I wasn't really looking at it, just trying to find something to do with my hands, and I couldn't believe it when I opened a card that Sarah must have posted only a day or so before. It was weird because she was never the sort of person who wrote to me – she was much more of a telephone girl. I burst into tears again as I read her innocent message: she'd included a cheque for my share of the prize money from Shifty's recent win and was suggesting we meet later that week for lunch. I clutched the card to me and hoped that wherever she was she was OK.

The funeral, some weeks later, was a really emotional time for everyone who had known Sarah. Pete couldn't come with me, so I went with my parents. When we got there, I wasn't surprised to find it was standing room only. I watched the service with Dandy and Sarah's housemate Ali, both of them absolutely gutted. As I watched her coffin being carried out, I was determined to make the very best of whatever time I had left. Driving home, I had one person on my mind – Pete.

In the long months that followed, I did everything I could to pull my marriage together. After an initial burst of attention, with Peter seeming like his old self, he soon returned to being as distant as when our problems had first surfaced. Whenever I went home – I was still driving up from London to be there every moment I could – he wasn't sleeping in our bed and our sex life had now completely died. I kept asking if he was seeing Samantha again, and he swore he wasn't, but something was definitely not right. What's wrong? I would ask. Is there anything I should know? Then one day he admitted that he'd met Samantha for a coffee in Leeds, where she was filming *Where the Heart Is*. I was furious and demanded to know why he'd met her after he'd promised me it was over. He said that it was only for a coffee and that they'd discussed his decision to leave *Emmerdale*, as he'd informed the producer that he wanted them to kill off Chris Tate.

'Why, Pete?' I asked. 'Why did you have to talk to *her* about it?'

'She was in the area and asked me to meet her, so I did,' he said, looking at the floor.

'So it's *not* over then, is it? I shouted, feeling like my heart was being ripped apart.

'It is,' he said, and walked out of the room.

I sat down, realising that, if he was meeting her 'just to talk', it was definitely not over. It would have been easier to believe their affair *was* over if he'd just met up with her and they'd slept together. I know this sounds odd, but sex is often just that – sex – whereas emotional attachment runs deeper; in my experience anyway. I let it go, hoping there was still a chance that he loved me enough to realise what he was throwing away.

The months passed and my brief elation at winning the

Best Actress award again for *Bad Girls* did nothing to dim the pain I felt, as I knew my marriage was dying. I still drove home every weekend – and Pete still went to the pub whenever I was due back. I kept trying to get him to talk to me, but we seemed to go round in circles. One rare day when we were both at home and Pete was in the living room reading the papers, I walked over and sat opposite him. He looked up at me with a curious expression on his face.

'Are you still sleeping with her? Tell me the truth,' I said, praying the answer was not the one I knew was coming.

He looked down at his paper and admitted that he was, but said that it had only just started again. I didn't believe him.

A week later, I received a phone call from my agent, David, saying that Pete and Samantha had been caught 'kissing' on camera by the *Daily Mirror* as they came out of a hotel in Leeds. The paper informed him that they would be printing the story on the front page the following day. I knew from the information that they'd given David that Pete's affair must have started again some time ago. I was devastated – now everyone would know, and the humiliation stung so badly.

The journalist had told David that in fact they had photos of them coming out of several hotels over as many months, so the affair had never really stopped.

I confronted Pete. 'They must have been following you for ages, as they wouldn't do a whole story on one meeting,' I said. In one way, I felt relieved to know I wasn't going mad and at least I knew why he was being the way he was with me. I knew I was beaten – I'd lost him. The immense sadness that my marriage to Peter was finished washed over me.

We sat in the kitchen the night before the *Daily Mirror* was to splash pictures of them kissing across the front page. 'Right, we've had our chance – it's over,' I said, looking at the man who'd stood opposite me at the altar and said he'd love me forever. He looked back at me with tears in his eyes and nodded. After he'd packed some bags, I walked out with him to the car. At the gate, we hugged and we both began to cry. I still loved him desperately but I would beg no more. I couldn't believe I might never feel his embrace again, then pulled myself away from his arms. As I watched him drive off, the knowledge that *she* was waiting for him in Windsor really hit me, and I walked towards our once happy home alone, knowing that this really was the end.

Back in the house, with Digger beside me and a glass of wine in my hand, I started to run over everything in my mind. Shit, I thought, I'm single and 40. Why, if he was going to leave me, couldn't it have been at 35? These thoughts were completely irrational. I knew Peter hadn't planned to do any of this to me – no one is perfect – but the deceit stung and every woman knows getting older is scary enough, but getting older alone seems even worse.

It did that day anyway.

'Oh, well,' I said to Digger as I filled my glass again. At least we've not had children, I thought, so no one else but me is hurting. But then again, maybe we'd have fought harder if we'd had kids – but now I'd never know. Both our sets of parents had been married for over 40 years and had stayed together. But we'd failed. My mind was filled with countless memories of happier times; only the wine I was drinking seemed to help still it. A few months earlier, I'd taken the decision to leave *Bad Girls*, so now I'd soon be out of a job as well as a relationship. I sat there feeling a strange numbness as my whole life seemed to crumble.

## 22

# The Worst Chapter of My Life

After Peter left, the months seemed to drag by endlessly. I was in the house alone, and as depression over the failure of our marriage set in, I was drinking more than was good for me, just trying to numb the pain. Work was slow too, but, after I'd sat at home for weeks waiting for the phone to ring, it finally did – with two jobs. Hurrah! I thought. At least they know I'm alive.

Work was just what I needed to keep my mind occupied. Brian Park had asked me to return to *Bad Girls* for three episodes of series six, to help the current Governor, Neil Grayling (brilliantly played by the lovely James Gaddas), bring down Fenner. Because I'd been rather hastily written out, with Fenner framing Karen for murder, I jumped at the chance. The fact that I didn't feel or look my best worked quite well, as Karen, with whom I'd previously felt very little affinity, was hiding out in her flat and drinking too much, trying to deal with betrayal by someone she'd been in love with. OK, so Pete hadn't framed me for murder! But I still felt pretty down.

After I'd shot my three episodes, things picked up a little and I became a jobbing actress again, appearing in the BBC's *Down to Earth* and *Holby City* and Channel 4's *Courtroom*. ITV didn't seem to want me; everything I went up for I didn't get, which was a double kick in the teeth after being disappointed about the post-*Emmerdale* contracts I'd been promised.

Oh well, I thought, no point dwelling. I'll just have to get on with it. Not long after this my agent called to tell me that Warren Clarke – I'd always loved him in *A Clockwork Orange* – had phoned to say he wanted me for an episode of BBC's *Dalziel and Pascoe*. I was very touched that he'd called direct and was thrilled at the prospect of working with him. After shooting our scenes in Scarborough we all went on a big boozathon. Along with John McArdle (who used to be Billy in *Brookside*), Warren, Colin Buchanan and my pal Sean McKenzie (who was filming *The Royal*, around the corner from us), I had 'a late one' in our hotel bar. It was nice to be out and forget my troubles for a while, but at 4am I left them to carry on all night.

The press were forever chasing me for a comment on why my marriage ended. I chose not to give any statements and did very little press apart from one 'At Home' shoot for *Hello!* magazine, where I tried to mask my pain by claiming that I was fine about everything that had happened. I could have made a lot more money if I'd slagged Pete off and gone into our personal details, but I still loved him and, although he was now living with Samantha, I felt he was missing me. He would ring my mobile to see how I was and his calls were becoming more and more frequent. But I'm the sort of person who wants things 100 per cent on the line before I'll take a chance, so there was no way I was going to ask him to come back in case he said no. I'd been humiliated enough.

Even though things were getting better work-wise, I just couldn't snap out of the numbness that had frozen me when Pete left. And I was still drinking too much, but that was the only thing that seemed to make me feel better.

I was very flattered when the jockey Fergal Lynch, whom I'd known on and off from racing and who often rode my horses, came into my personal life. To have a younger man – and a lot younger at that, as he was 26 – giving me attention was uplifting. Our relationship wasn't serious but it was fun and it helped me keep my head above water. We had some good laughs and some good times and even spent the day at Joe and Jack Berry's annual charity barbecue with my parents, who liked Fergal, but after a few months it fizzled out and we became friends. It was too soon after Pete to be looking for a serious relationship.

Later that year, Fergal and his brother Sean invited me to the Breeders' Cup in Santa Anita. I'd finished filming and hadn't had a break in ages, plus my great mate Clare was still living there, so it would give me the chance to meet up with her for the first time in ages. So I said yes, and we also made arrangements to fly on to Australia afterwards for the Melbourne Cup.

We stayed in LA for four days and I bumped into Kieren Fallon, who was over there riding Islington in the fillies' and mares' turf race. He won and that night we celebrated at Gary Stevens's house. Gary, who is a champion jockey in America and recently starred in the film *Seabiscuit*, had a gorgeous home, which was soon packed with people who intended to party all night long. About 4am, I went back to the hotel with Kieren, Fergal, Sean and Clare, and as the sun came up I lay in bed thinking what a great time I'd had. I was determined not to let myself fall back into a rut when I got home. I was living again and it felt good.

A couple of days later, all of us except Fergal, who was meeting a friend, flew to Melbourne, checked into our hotel and were soon living it large. Sean and I did the wine region around Melbourne and spent two days pissed! It was scorching hot on the day of the Cup, which was won by Makybe Diva (soon to score a hat trick over the next three years). The rest of the trip flew by; it was fun but I was happy to get home.

Not long before I left Australia, my agent had called and left a message saying I had a casting at ITV, of all places, for a show called *Donovan*, starring Tom Conti. Tom Conti, eh? I thought. I'd admired him ever since *Shirley Valentine* and the idea of working with him in a proper drama really appealed. I flew back home and, after a quick read-through with the production team, I was promptly offered the part of Sally Parker, a woman under suspicion of murdering her husband. Kim would be proud, I said to myself, as I collected the scripts and headed for the Manchester location.

The cast were staying at the Malmaison in Piccadilly and one night I was lying in bed around 2am when the hotel's fire alarm suddenly went off. Just what I need now! I thought, as I waited for it to stop. When I realised it wasn't going to, I quickly got dressed and exited the hotel via the fire escape! Outside, where most of the guests had gathered in their nightwear, I noticed that Tom and I were the only ones fully dressed and he'd brought his laptop while I had my suitcase. No one could have accused us of not being cool under fire.

I'd only just wrapped [finished] shooting on *Donovan* when my agent called to say I'd been offered a role in a BBC afternoon play, *The Good Citizen*, with Claire Goose. I'd also just ridden in and won a charity race at Windsor for the Princess Royal Trust for Carers, organised by Leslie Graham of Channel Four Racing. I was thrilled to win and was just beginning to think my luck was finally on the up, when things took several turns for the worse.

On 29 August 2004, my horse King's Rock was running at Beverley. He was trained by Kevin Ryan and I'd been riding him out once or twice a week when I wasn't filming. Neil Callan rode a great race on him and won, but unfortunately he was then claimed for £10,000 – which meant I'd now lost my favourite horse. To cheer myself up, I went for a day's racing at Pontefract, where I bumped into Kieren Fallon. I hadn't seen him since LA and after a brief chat we made our way to the car park, as we were both leaving. Kieren's car wouldn't start, so he asked me to phone the AA for him. I waited until they arrived and we quickly struck up our usual flirty banter, but for some reason I found myself more attracted to him than I had been before.

The AA guys couldn't fix Kieren's car and towed it away, so he asked me if I could drive him to Newmarket, as he was riding out first thing in the morning. I agreed and on the way there he told me how he'd separated from his wife and was staying with a friend. The message was clear – we wanted each other. We drove in silence to his friend's house and went on to enjoy a night of wild passion. It was fantastic for both of us, but when morning broke we knew we'd made a mistake in taking our friendship over the line, and agreed that it would be a one-off.

Not long after this my horse King's Empire, trained by Declan Carroll, broke a leg at Southwell and had to be put down. I threw myself into filming on location and tried to put it out of my mind. The shoot was easy and everyone was pleasant, but the script was a bit complex and I couldn't really understand what the story was about. I just 'winged it' and hoped it would make sense to me when I saw it on screen.

On the last day of filming, I received a call from a man who was going to make the heartache I'd suffered over the past year seem like a bed of roses. I was walking back from the set when my mobile rang with a call from a number I didn't recognise. When I answered, a Scottish voice replied. (I'm not putting his name in this book – he's already had his 15 minutes of fame out of me.)

'Hello, Claire – you won't remember me but I met you a few years ago on the *Emmerdale* set – I was with Malandra Burrows.'

'Oh, hi,' I said, not having a clue who he was.

'We swapped numbers and you told me to give you a call sometime to discuss punting,' he said.

When he said 'punting', even though I'd clearly forgotten him, it sounded like the sort of thing I might say, so I had no reason to doubt we'd met before. He went on to say we had mutual friends in racing, and that we should hook up and do some betting together because he'd heard I had a talent for it. You're probably thinking this all sounds suspicious, but I was flattered, as horses are my passion, and I listened as he suggested that, to show he knew what he was talking about, he'd give me a tip that I was to 'lump on' – put a large amount of money on it to win.

Now, as someone who normally only made bets of £20 to £40 and had only two betting accounts, the Tote and Victor Chandler, I saw betting large amounts as risky. But the suggestion was also quite exciting, so I called my bookie and managed to get £500 on the horse, split between the two accounts. I listened out for the result later that day and was more than a little surprised when the horse came fourth. Confused, I called the man. 'Why did you give me that dodgy tip? He quite clearly wasn't going to win and now I'm £500 down. What the hell did you do that for?' I said, absolutely furious.

'Don't worry, Claire, I'll give you double your money back when you're in London.'

If it wasn't for the fact that I knew I was going to be in London the next week for Brian Park's birthday party, I would have written off the money – and him – and moved on. But why should I lose out just to let someone else make a fool out of me? I thought, so I arranged to meet him the following week – which in hindsight was the biggest mistake I've ever made.

On the day of Brian's party, I was at my London flat wrapping gifts for him when the mobile rang. It was *him*. He said that he had my money and asked if I could meet him at Browns restaurant in Islington at 8pm. I asked if he could make it any earlier, as I had a party to go to, but he said he couldn't. Not wanting to lose out, I agreed. Later, at 7.15, when I was just about to order a cab, he called again. 'Sorry, Claire, I'm running late. I still haven't got back from the races. Can you make it 10pm?' I explained that that would make me late but he said he couldn't make it any earlier and, against my better judgement, I said I'd meet him at 10pm.

At 9.30, I received a text saying, 'I'm on my way, but I'll be closer to your place in Stoke Newington [I didn't notice at the time that he knew what area I lived in], so why don't I drop the money off there?'

It seemed like an easy option, as it meant I could leave the money at home rather than take it to the party with me. After giving him the address, I called my friend Pete Newman, who lived near by and had been my driver on *Down to Earth*. 'Pete, can you do me a favour and nip round for an hour,' I said, 'as I've got this guy I don't know dropping some money off for me and I don't feel comfortable being here alone.'

Pete arrived ten minutes later. We had a drink and waited. And waited. And waited.

After another hour – it was now nearly 10.30pm – I called his mobile, which put me through to an answering machine, and moments later a text beeped back: 'Can't speak but am on way.' Another hour had passed, by which time I was so late for the party and in such a foul mood that it hardly seemed worth going, when he called saying he couldn't make it after all and asking if we could meet in the morning. I lost my temper and told him, in front of Pete, that he could just fuck off and keep the money, and stop wasting my time, before slamming the phone down.

Pete left a while later and I stomped off to bed with a stress headache, missing the party. I didn't hear from him for a few days and was back home in Yorkshire when the next text came through: 'I'm really sorry about what happened, Claire – let me make it up to you.' I ignored it and the following three over as many days. Then I read what he had texted: 'Look I've been a prat – put a bet for yourself on these horses and you'll make back what I owe and more – sorry.' I didn't put a bet on but I did check the results later that day. All of them had won. Hmm, I thought, he's a bit odd but he does seem to know his racing.

When another text came through the next day with another tip, I placed a modest bet without texting him back to say I'd done so. It won. He called me later that day from a withheld number – if I'd known it was him, I wouldn't have answered – and asked me if I'd enjoyed the tips. I should have put the phone down but found myself talking to him as he apologised again for 'messing you about'. It wasn't intentional, he said, adding that, hopefully, I'd made my money back by now and should be able to see that he knew what he was talking about. He impressed me with what I can only describe as expert knowledge of national hunt racing. I found myself strangely convinced that I should give him another chance when he assured me, 'If we got together, we would make a lot of money, Claire.'

Over the next few weeks, I placed several bets from his tips, all of which won. And my own horse, Creskeld, won a decent handicapped race. It was very good prize money, which cheered me up no end. He then suggested that, as we were doing so well, we should open some more accounts with bookies, so we could place larger bets. Caught up with the excitement of making decent money and having heard nothing from my agent in quite some time, I went along with this suggestion and opened three new accounts. I would then stake the money, he would send the tip and when the horse won I would transfer half the winnings to him.

We were making quite good money and he hadn't messed me about again for several months, so, the next time I was down in London, for a meeting with my agent, and he suggested we meet for dinner, I agreed. I turned up at Browns half-expecting 'Mr Mystery' not to turn up, but as I was being shown to my seat I saw an average-looking man in his thirties waiting for me. I hadn't asked him what he looked like – this wasn't a date – but because he had a rather nice voice I had somehow imagined him to be better-looking. 'Hi, Claire. Glad you could make it,' he said, as I sat down next to him. After a few drinks, we had dinner and I found myself warming to his slightly roguish charm. He apologised again for what he called 'a misunderstanding' over the initial bet, but we agreed that we were now doing well and should go on working together.

Back in Yorkshire, I continued placing the bets as he continued sending the tips. The next few weeks passed by quite uneventfully until one day he called and said, 'Right – we've had a good run with small bets. It's time we upped the stakes. I've got a dead cert on a horse to win at Kempton. Put a large bet on it to win.'

'A large bet!' I said. 'Are you nuts?'

'Trust me, Claire, I've got inside information on this one – it will win.'

The next morning, I nervously placed the bet, spreading it over all the accounts. I spent the day working from home, answering fan mail that had built up, and later that afternoon I watched the race, only to see our horse fall three furlongs out – and our money go down the drain. My heart sank. When I called him, he made light of the loss, saying, 'Don't worry, we've only lent it to them. We'll win it back. If you want to make serious money, you have to take risks. It's just a blip.'

Trying to see the bigger picture, I accepted what he was saying and asked him if he would transfer his half of the lost stake into my account. He promised he would in two weeks, once he'd been paid.

Nearly all the following bets I placed lost. And within ten days of the first horse falling nearly every other horse he tipped failed and we'd now lost a large amount of money in lost stakes. He assured me that he would 'sort me out' as soon as he had a chance and that we were just having 'a bad run' but we should stick at it, as our luck would soon change. I told him that I couldn't afford to place any more bets, as I wasn't working and had had to clear the debts we'd already run up. 'OK,' he said, 'we'll use my account and I'll place the next ones.'

Over the next few weeks, he placed all our bets, selected together by phone and text, and, as he'd predicted, our luck did change and we earned quite a bit of money. When we next had a fairly large win, he offered to transfer my half of the winnings from his account to mine over the next few days. For several days, he stalled and stalled, blaming everything: the banks, the betting company and even 'personal problems' connected to his mother's illness. I was at the end of my tether, as the money I'd paid out to clear our losses had hit me hard and I was now desperate to recoup it. After he ignored my texts and calls for two whole days I was beginning to think he'd done a runner and that I'd lost my money.

But I had to put it all out of my mind as I went to pay tribute at the funeral of Stan Richards, my dear former co-star on *Emmerdale*. At the church, I cried for the loss of a lovely man and for the mess my life had turned into. My husband had left me; my career seemed to have hit the skids; I'd somehow got myself involved with a man who appeared to have taken me for a financial ride; I was drinking too much again as a consequence of these events, which seemed to be relentless, and I'd even turned to cocaine occasionally – something I'd never done even in my youth. I wasn't addicted but I found the odd line helped lift my mood, although I soon decided that, even though there was still some left in the house, I was not going to do that again. However hard my life was, I knew I was better than that.

The day after the funeral, I was home alone, having had several glasses of wine, when *he* called. 'I'm really sorry, Claire, that I've not been in touch but I've been in hospital. I was mugged.'

'Oh,' I said, not sure if I could believe a word he was saying. But, being a trusting person, I couldn't bring myself to doubt his story.

'Anyway, I'm on my way up to your place now. I'm on the train. Let's sort this money situation out once and for all,' he said, catching me off guard. The last thing I wanted in the world right now was to have him in my house, but the opportunity to get my money back made me agree to the visit. Two hours later, he arrived, handing me two bottles of red wine and saying, 'Peace offering.'

By now, I was too tired and full of feelings to bring the money up. I'll just leave it for him to mention and hopefully he's got a cheque with him, I hoped, as I passed him the corkscrew and he poured me a large glass of wine.

We sat well apart on the sofa. He said that he had had the money for me but that when he'd been mugged he'd had to cancel his chequebook and was waiting for a new one. 'Why didn't you just do a bank transfer, like I did?' I asked him and suddenly found myself bursting into tears. I'd let him into my home and he didn't even have my money for me. All the emotion of the past few weeks seemed to spill out and I could barely find the words to tell him how let down I felt by this constant disappointment. He moved to my end of the sofa and put his arm around me.

'Don't cry – I'm here for you,' he said.

I wanted to smash him in the face and scream that he was my biggest problem, but somehow the comfort of being in someone's arms seemed to take away my anger. But when he leaned over to kiss me I pulled away. 'No, don't,' I told him.

'I'm just trying to cheer you up. You've been through a rough time, Claire, but I'm here for you,' he said, as he filled my wineglass and passed it to me, then gestured to where the old package of cocaine was lying by the stereo.

'Why don't you have some of that? It'll make you feel better.'

'No,' I said. 'I don't want to.'

'Go on,' he urged. 'It's only coke – it'll liven you up and make you feel a bit happier.'

254

I knew I really shouldn't but I was so drunk, emotional and not thinking straight that I soon found myself snorting a line of cocaine as he smiled, telling me that I'd feel better in a minute. As I finished the line, I noticed he had his mobile in his hand. 'I'm just sending a text,' he said. I had no idea at the time, but he was filming me on his phone. I was being set up.

As the cocaine took hold of me, I seemed to lose control and before I knew it his hands were everywhere. Because of the drug, I no longer felt the same repulsion towards him and I found myself responding. We ended up in bed and afterwards I passed out. The next morning I woke up with a thumping head, to find his arms around me. He kissed me and I jumped out of bed, ran to the bathroom and was violently sick. Oh, God, what have I done? I thought, as I retched over the toilet bowl. After I'd wiped my face I walked back into the bedroom, pulling my dressing gown tightly around me. He beckoned me to join him on the bed.

'I think you should leave,' I said. 'I've made a mistake.'

'What do you mean?' he shouted, as I walked out of the bedroom.

He dressed and quickly followed me downstairs into the kitchen.

'Look, I didn't mean to do that last night and I don't feel well. Do you mind leaving me, as I want to be alone?' I said, my head spinning. How on earth had it come to this?

Ignoring what I'd said, he just sat on the sofa and started reeling off his plans for what we could do with our futures.

Infuriated, I made it very clear I didn't want a relationship with him.

He stood up and walked over to me in the kitchen, his face full of anger. 'Who the fuck do think you are?' he screamed, as he leaned into my space. My face must have shown fear, because he backed off and apologised. He said he understood and that we could 'just be friends', then asked me to drive him to the station, saying he'd call me about the money later that week. I quickly dropped him off and then drove straight home and sat in my bath until the water was cold. The cheque never came, of course, but a series of late-night calls did.

I locked myself away at home and stopped going out. Each night, he'd fill my answering machine – or my ear if I answered when my guard was down – with bizarre reasons why he didn't have my money. As his rambling excuses continued, I began to worry for my own safety. I'd let someone into my life who appeared to be disturbed, but I was too embarrassed to tell anyone what was happening. I just felt so stupid. I couldn't take the stress of speaking to him any more and stopped taking any unknown calls altogether, but the text messages continued.

Over the next few months, CDs, love poems, phone calls and more sinister text and picture messages came through, and by this time I was saving them all. At first, I tried to ignore them, but by August 2005 they were becoming frightening. One read: 'The gloves are off now Claire.' Another: 'Ur history, goodnight Vienna.' The night one came through reading: 'No more Mr Nice Guy. Let's get the rules sorted right now,' I lost my cool and called him, determined to put an end to this once and for all. He ignored my call and I left a message on his answering machine telling him – in no uncertain terms – that unless he left me alone I would go to the police.

I didn't hear anything from him for a few days and was just beginning to hope that he'd gone away, when one night I was lying in bed around 1am and the phone beeped. I was half-asleep when I clicked the phone open to see a short video clip of myself taking the line of cocaine on the night he'd been at my house and it became clear to me at that moment that he had secretly been filming me. Along with the video were the words: '£10,000 by Monday the 15th of August or the video goes to the papers.'

What was left of my world – and, by now, my sanity – was ripped apart. I was being blackmailed.

# 23

# Fighting Back

I stayed in my bedroom for 24 hours trying to work out what to do. I could give this man the money he was demanding in the hope that he'd go away for good, but I felt certain that would never happen. There was only one choice: to contact the press myself to explain what was happening to me and by doing so take away the only power he had.

The thought made me feel sick. I'd never revealed much of my private life to the press, even when the interest was huge, and now I was contemplating calling a national newspaper and admitting that I was being blackmailed because I'd been videoed taking cocaine. What a mess, I thought, ashamed that I'd been so stupid to have let him or the drug anywhere near me. I just wanted to run away and hide, but when you find yourself trapped like this there are only two ways to go. You either go down, which in my case meant surrendering to this man who wanted to control my life and take away everything I'd worked so hard for. Or you come out fighting. I chose to fight.

I'd met Suzanne Kerins, the top showbiz reporter at the *Sunday Mirror*, recently at a film premiere and had been really impressed by how nice she seemed – a quality I'd found quite rare in tabloid gossip columnists. Whenever she'd written about me, which had been quite a bit since Pete left me, her pieces were always positive – if sometimes a little personal – so I decided that she was the person I wanted to break the story to in my attempt to get myself out of the hell I was in.

It was 2am when I texted a very close friend who knew Suzanne, asking him to give her my number and get her to call me a.s.a.p. My friend texted back that he would and if I wanted to talk to him I could call. He realised there was something seriously wrong for me to send a text like that, but he knew me well enough to do as I asked and not push me for my reasons.

I got up and walked around the house, checking all the windows and doors were locked, grabbed a bottle of wine and took it back to bed with me. Digger followed me around; he knew there was something wrong and never left my side. I got into bed and lay back in the dark as my mind whirred. What will my parents think? Will the scandal stop me from working again? Will I have to go to court and reveal how stupid I've been? I was devastated at the thought of causing my parents any upset. Dad's health was bad and Mum had her work cut out looking after him.

The last thing they needed now was the news that their daughter was caught in a drugs scandal – the village would be talking about it for weeks.

I pulled the sheets up around me and tried to sleep. The mobile kept beeping text messages over and over again – it was him. I switched it off and threw it on the floor, then burst into tears and eventually cried myself to sleep. The home phone woke me at 10.30am and I knocked the empty wine bottle over as I reached out to answer it.

'Hi, Claire?' said the female voice.

'Yes,' I said, wondering who it was.

'It's Suzanne Kerins from the *Sunday Mirror*. Are you OK to talk?'

I gripped the phone as I sat upright. There was no turning back now, I realised. I lit a cigarette and began to tell Suzanne the whole sordid saga.

I was surprised by how empowering it felt to be talking to someone about it and I immediately felt the anger rise that I had even been forced to do this. Once I'd told her everything, Suzanne said she thought I'd had a terrible ordeal. The fact that I'd taken the occasional line of cocaine to cheer myself up after my marriage had broken down was stupid, she said, but the hell I'd been put through at the hands of someone who had deliberately targeted a vulnerable woman was much, much worse.

She explained that the *Sunday Mirror* were completely on my side and if I wanted to talk they would set up a 'sting' in London where I would call him on my mobile while they listened in and recorded the conversation of him blackmailing me. We agreed that I would get the train down in the next few days and she would pick me up from King's Cross. We would then go somewhere quiet to record the mobile conversation that would prove I was being blackmailed.

After finishing the call, I lay back wondering if I'd made the right decision. I turned the mobile back on to find several threatening messages from him demanding 'money or else' and I knew I had to go through with it.

I decided I'd do the interview and the phone call first and then tell my parents when I went home. Throughout the day, new messages came through on the mobile, all from him. One said that if I didn't put £1,000 into his account today he would sell his phone to the highest bidder. I called Suzanne, worried that he would sell the photos before I could explain what had really happened. After reassuring me there was no need to panic she went off to speak to her team at the paper and said she would call me back. When she rang, she told me it had been decided that the best thing to do was for me to continue to pay him, but to tell him that I would not be able to get the full £10,000 he wanted until next Monday and until then I would put the £1,000 in his account to show that I was complying with his rules. I didn't want to put another penny in the scumbag's account but I knew it was the best thing to do.

I transferred the money and then another £500 he had demanded as 'a show of faith', and a couple of days later set off to meet Suzanne in London. She picked me up in a cab and she was warm and made me feel relaxed. We went to the Groucho Club in Soho and, as I said hello to the receptionists, I thought, A lot of things have gone on in the rooms upstairs but I bet this isn't normally one of them. Once I was installed in the room, the phone was tapped, so that when I called him it would record both sides of the conversation. The room was tiny and I felt quite claustrophobic – which was probably panic setting in. Suzanne connected the phone to a Dictaphone and told me to stay on as long as possible. When I asked her if the machine was silent, as I didn't want him to realise what was going on, she assured me it was. I called his number and the tape began to record. This is part of the transcript that went to the police:

Man: I am stood outside in the fucking middle of the street. Bring me the money now.
Claire King: Look, I said it will be in on Monday. You said the deal was to get it on the 15th. I've said I will get it to you. I have already given you £1,500.
M: Lack of communication, Claire – always a fucking problem. You don't seem to grasp that.
CK: I asked you not to contact me until I've got the money. You said I could have the phone if I paid you the grand. I paid you the grand but I didn't get the phone. You said you'd post it. Then you wanted another five hundred. And that I now owe you £8,500 for the phone with the pictures on it of me taking cocaine. And I didn't get it.
M: Claire, let's put a fucking end to this now. If you don't do this, you are fucked.

CK: What do you mean?

M: Come down here right now. Right fucking here now. I will show you the fucking videophone. You are not getting it. But I will show you it.

CK: How do I know you are going to be there? You haven't turned up before. Do you promise to give me that phone if I come to meet you then?

M: No, you can see it. You are not getting it until I get the money.

CK: Why?

M: Because as soon as you have that then I have no leg to stand on. No way. You can see it but you are not getting it.

CK: You could have copied it on to other phones. You could blackmail me again. It's twice you have done it. How do I know you are not going to do it again? You could be lying. You have lied about everything else so far.

M: I could be lying but I don't give a shit what you think. If you want to come and see it, come and see it. I am not giving you the phone without any money. No way.

CK: What are you going to do with it if the money is late?

M: Now you're telling me it is going to be late?

CK: I'm swearing it will be in on Monday. I don't want this in the papers. I don't want my parents reading about it. You know that. How can I guarantee that you are not going to do this again? Are you going to write a note saying that you're not going to blackmail me any more and that is it?

M: Yes. Come down here now with £500.

CK: Where am I going to get it? I haven't got any money on me.

M: Well, I suggest you pick out a certain loan shark then.

CK: I'm scared. I want this to finish. I want it to be at an end. I told you I'd have the remaining of the blackmail money in on Monday. And that's it; finished.

M: If you use that word blackmail again I will swing for you.

CK: Well, what else is it then? What do you call it if it's not blackmail?

M: Negotiations.

After the call I was shaking with nerves – I hated even speaking to him at this point – we went to the nearby hotel where I had to pose for pictures to go along with the 'confessional'. I hadn't even thought about having to do that and the last thing I wanted was to pose on a sofa showing how rundown it had all made me; but I understood that that is how papers do these things.

After we'd done the photos, Suzanne interviewed me 'properly', covering everything from beginning to end. I felt so embarrassed admitting everything from the intimate details of text messages we'd exchanged, the details of the night he'd stayed over and the humiliation of the terror I'd experienced at the hands of a blackmailer. I was so pleased that she was the person helping me. I really felt, and hoped, I could trust her, as she seemed to be on my side, but it was still soul-destroying to reveal how stupid I was to get mixed up with such a person.

Suzanne assured me that the article would be as sensitive as possible but told me to be aware that the headline would probably be sensationalist and the story would fill the front page. I knew I had no control over what went into the story, but I'd told the truth and they'd listened to the phone call and photographed the text messages, so at least it gave me a chance to put my side across before he could sell his. Plus, as they'd now heard him blackmailing me, it would no longer be my word against his, which he'd threatened would be the case.

I'd been advised to maintain minimal contact with him until the story broke on Sunday, so as to preserve the illusion that I was going to pay him the £8,500 on the Monday. But, as Suzanne knew I was now getting very stressed and didn't feel safe home alone, she arranged for me to fly out to Belfast for a few days and come back when the story had appeared. I went home to pack and phoned my parents to ask if they'd have Digger for a few days, which they agreed to do. I drove the short distance – it felt like a hundred miles – to their house, knowing I would have to tell them everything before the paper came out.

After pulling up outside, I sat in the car and lit a cigarette. God, what are they going to say? I worried as I got Digger out and walked up to the house. This would be the hardest thing I'd ever have to say, but I just hoped they'd understand what a mess I'd got myself in and not judge me for it. As soon as I was in the house, Mum asked me what was wrong. 'I've been really stupid,' I said, as I lit a cigarette and began to tell them the whole story.

Neither Mum nor Dad chastised me for the situation I was in; they just wished I'd told them sooner. They agreed that I'd been set up and promised to stand by me. I was touched, and that afternoon there were many hugs and tears.

The text messages continued once I was in Belfast. Because I was ignoring his calls – it was now Saturday and I couldn't bear to speak to him again – they had become even more sinister. 'Uve let me down. I am going 2 sell my phone to the highest bidder 2day,' one read, but I knew that unless he had already done it earlier in the week, I had beaten him to it. In 12 hours' time, the Sunday papers would drop through letterboxes throughout the country and it would all be over – or at least that is what I told myself as I had drinks with Mary Rose, a friend who I had met in Belfast when she was managing a nightclub there. She now had her own bar and restaurant called the Factory, and it was there that we met and tried to take my mind off the millions of people who would be reading about my mistakes over their cornflakes the following day.

When the paper was delivered to my room on the Sunday morning, my face stared back at me from the front page, beneath the headline: 'Claire King: My Cocaine Shame'. Jesus! I thought. Anyone would think I was some kind of addict. Luckily, when I opened it and read the following two pages I could see the article was very well balanced and didn't match the headline. They had even contacted *him*. 'I have never blackmailed Claire. I've never demanded money from her,' he said.

Ha! I thought. You've obviously no idea that they taped a half-hour call proving you've done just that.

The rest of the day flew by, with my phone constantly ringing, as people called to check I was OK and tell me they were on my side. Even my parents called to say it was fine and Pete left me a message of concern, but I couldn't bear to speak to him just yet. As I got dressed and prepared to meet Mary Rose for lunch, I knew I couldn't hide away, as I was front-page news, but it was over in my mind.

During lunch, lots of people passed us smiling sympathetically; they were on my side. As Mary Rose put it to one journalist who turned up once word was out that I was in Belfast, 'She made a mistake – but she didn't hurt anyone but herself.'

And she was right. I had made a mistake and I would never make one like that again. But right then and there I didn't care. It was over. I was free.

# 24

# New Beginnings

It's February 2006 and I'm just wondering how to finish the last chapter of this book and still in shock that I've written it at all. Peter has moved back in. We're not together but he's split with Samantha and, as it's a pretty big house (which is just as well, because my friend Ali has moved into one of the spare rooms), it didn't seem right to say no. Besides, Digger's happy that his daddy's home – although, due to his current theatre commitments, neither of us is sure how long he's staying.

Writing this book has been a journey I never expected to make. The five months since my life was splashed across the tabloids have been a real eye-opener, to say the least. I was deeply touched by the thousands of letters of support I received. Thank you to all those people – it has really meant so much to me.

The first time I went out after it all happened was to the

races at York with my parents, my friend Ann Duffield and Russ and Debs, two recent pals who've shown me great loyalty. I was really nervous as we entered the owners' and trainers' bar, but I needn't have been because the entire bar staff gave me a round of applause and a bottle of champagne on the house. Everyone was so positive and I can honestly say I've not received one negative comment from anyone who counts – you certainly learn who your friends are when the chips are down.

Because I'd not been acting for a while, I decided to immerse myself in my other passion – horses. Creskeld had moved back to his old trainer, Les Eyre, so I flew out to Spain to spend some time with Les and his family and spent every day riding out in the beautiful surroundings with his daughter Charlotte – I'm tipping her to be a top female jockey of the future. The Spanish heat made such a lovely change from the cold Yorkshire mornings that I even decided to buy a villa near by, so I'm looking forward to having plenty of fun in the sun this year.

I hope Creskeld's move to Spain will do him good, as I'm now down to my last three horses, having bought a share of a new horse called Fremen, trained by Dandy Nicholls, and a three-year-old unraced colt trained by Declan Carroll called King of Rhythm. Fingers crossed that 2006 will be their year.

Having another woman in the house has worked out well, as Ali enjoys her racing too. We've had many girly weekends away, including the Breeders' Cup in New York and a fabulous trip to Paris for the Prix de l'Arc de Triomphe. It's good to be getting out and about again and I'm enjoying the attention being a newly single woman brings.

Recently I got the call to play a defence barrister on *Hollyoaks*, which was just what I needed to get 'back in the loop', and after filming it I even managed to help produce (and star in, naturally!) a short film called *Your Place or Mine?*, which will soon be doing the rounds at the festivals. It was really nice to have a hand in the creative process rather than just be the usual hired help. I've also just completed an episode of a new murder mystery series, *Mayo*, for the BBC alongside Alistair McGowan and have several exciting projects in the pipeline. All in all, work seems to be on the up and suddenly I've found myself in demand for countless health and beauty features – God knows what they'd think if they could see me in the morning! But when the call comes who's going to say no?

I really don't know what's in store for me next. As you'll have gathered by now, my life seems to be like one big soap opera, so maybe I'll rejoin one soon. Or maybe not. Watch this space.

# Picture Credits